SOUTHERN
ROCKY MOUNTAIN
Wildflowers

A FIELD GUIDE TO
COMMON WILDFLOWERS, SHRUBS,
AND TREES

Text by Leigh Robertson

Photos by Duane B. Squires and others

FALCON®

HELENA, MONTANA

ROCKY MOUNTAIN
NATURE ASSOCIATION

A FALCON GUIDE ®

Falcon® is continually expanding its list of recreational guidebooks. All books include detailed descriptions, accurate maps, and all the information necessary for enjoyable trips. You can order extra copies of this book and get information and prices for other Falcon® guidebooks by writing Falcon, P.O. Box 1718, Helena, MT 59624 or calling toll-free 1-800-582-2665. Please ask for a free copy of our current catalog. Visit our website at www.FalconOutdoors.com or contact us by e-mail at falcon@falconguide.com.

CAUTION

All participants in the recreational activities suggested by this book must assume responsibility for their own actions and safety. The information contained in this guidebook cannot replace sound judgment and good decision-making skills, which help reduce risk exposure; nor does the scope of this book allow for disclosure of all the potential hazards and risks involved in such activities.

Learn as much as possible about the recreational activities in which you participate, prepare for the unexpected, and be cautious. The reward will be a safer and more enjoyable experience.

CONTENTS

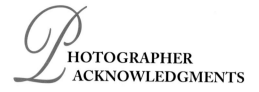PHOTOGRAPHER ACKNOWLEDGMENTS

Duane B. Squires (1924–1987) was an educator, outdoorsman, and avid amateur nature photographer. The Iowa native and long-time Boulder and Longmont, Colorado, elementary school principal was a member of the Photographic Society of America, St. Vrain Photographic Society, and the Rocky Mountain Nature Association.

Mr. Squires used his camera to express his affection for the beauty he encountered in the Rocky Mountain West after moving to Colorado in 1954. His photographs have been donated for this publication courtesy of his wife, Bonnie, of Longmont, and his daughters, Debbie and Cathy, both of Boulder.

Thanks also go to Joan Childers, Mari Coen, and Judy Visty, Rocky Mountain National Park staff members who helped make available photographs from the park collection. Also contributing generously was the Helen Fowler Library at Denver Botanic Gardens.

Several slides appearing in this volume come from the collections of Golden, Colorado, photographer Loraine Yeatts, who also assisted in accuracy verification of all species in the book, and H. Wayne Phillips, Great Falls, Montana. Other photographers featured are Rocky Mountain National Park interpretive staff member Leanne Benton; Richard Beidleman, professor of biology (emeritus) at The Colorado College in Colorado Springs; and George Hockman, a long-time interpretive ranger at Rocky Mountain National Park.

AUTHOR'S ACKNOWLEDGMENTS

For their suggestions, I would like to thank Tass Kelso, The Colorado College, and the staff members of the Bear Creek Nature Center in Colorado Springs.

My editor and this book's project coordinator, John Gunn of the Rocky Mountain Nature Association, was always upbeat, encouraging, and very helpful. It was a pleasure working with him. His efforts were aided greatly by Rocky Mountain National Park interpreter Leanne Benton, whose expertise helped produce the list of flowering plants identified in this book and contributed greatly to manuscript review.

I am especially grateful to George Cameron, botany instructor at Pikes Peak Community College, for his technical review of the manuscript, recommendations, and expert advice. Thanks also to Colorado Springs Park and Recreation Department and El Paso County Parks Department volunteers Jerry and Serann Duncan for their excellent plant list and to Megan Hiller, Erin Turner, Tom Marino, and Arik Ohnstad, who directed the efforts at Falcon Publishing. H. Wayne Phillips also contributed to the book's editorial content.

Most importantly, I would like to express by heartfelt appreciation to my husband, Michael Fuston, and daughter, Megan, for their support. They graciously gave me the time and space to conduct research and write this book.

Finally, I would like to thank the people who have helped inspire my love of wildflowers: Ann Zwinger and Beatrice Willard, whose wonderful book, *The Land Above the Trees*, transports readers to the alpine tundra; Dr. Gary Mullins for encouraging me to become an interpreter; author Peggy Parr and volunteer Frank Brunk, my high-altitude Pikes Peak friends; and my parents, Alec and Esther, for taking Linda, Neil, and me on hikes to many beautiful places.

Leigh Robertson

THE SOUTHERN
ROCKY MOUNTAIN REGION

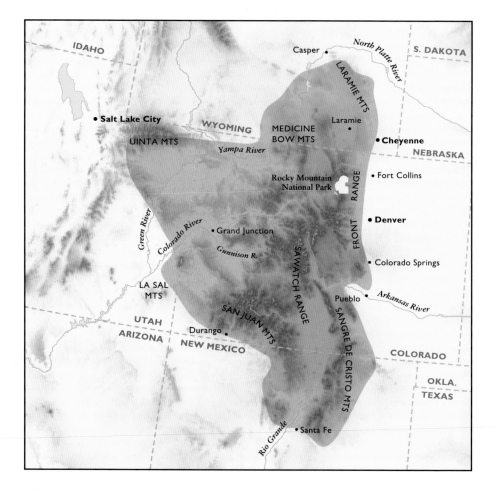

INTRODUCTION

A Wondrous Variety of Wildflowers

"Climb the mountains and get their good tidings. Nature's peace will flow into you as sunshine flows into trees. The winds will blow their own freshness into you, and the storms their energy, while cares will drop off like autumn leaves."
—*John Muir*

"The earth laughs in flowers..."—*Ralph Waldo Emerson*

Who can forget their favorite Southern Rocky Mountain scenes? Perhaps your memory is of the diamond-shaped east face of Longs Peak in Rocky Mountain National Park or the snowy Medicine Bow Mountains of Wyoming. Maybe it is of the jagged crests of the Sangre de Cristos, the solitary mass of Pikes Peak, or Utah's wild Uintas. Memories of favorite places in the Southern Rockies are like old friends—far away, perhaps, but always dear to the heart.

Mental snapshots of mountains usually capture forbidding, rugged alpine sentinels. But in between the snows of spring and fall, grand displays of wildflowers soften any harshness as nature generously cloaks the Southern Rockies in a dazzling gown of colors.

This flower guide is intended to introduce you to many of the more common—and more beloved—wildflowers of the Southern Rocky Mountains. The region covered in this book ranges from the Laramie Mountains in southern Wyoming south to the Sangre de Cristo Mountains of New Mexico, from the Front Range of Colorado's Rockies west to the mountains of eastern Utah.

The Southern Rockies is an amazingly diverse region, with many delights awaiting the ardent explorer. The great variety of rock, soil types, elevations, and climates provides habitats for an abundance of plants and animals. Botanists estimate that there are more than 3,000 species of flowering plants and conifers in Colorado alone. The wildflowers range in size from the ground-hugging Alpine Nailwort to thirteen-foot-high sunflowers. The colors are as varied as the paints on an artist's palette.

This multiplicity of blossoms is found in regions commonly referred to as ecosystems, or life zones. Ecosystems are defined as recognizable communities of plants and animals affected by environmental factors such as elevation, wind, temperature, precipitation, sunlight, soil type, and direction of slope.

In the Southern Rockies, temperatures cool as elevation increases. On average, the temperature drops three degrees (Fahrenheit) for every 1,000 feet gained. As elevations rise and temperatures cool, precipitation generally increases. Also changing, in direct response to changes in climate, is plant life.

It is commonly said that to gain 1,000 feet in elevation is similar to traveling 600 miles north, meaning climatic conditions and plants encountered on the highest peaks resemble those found in the Arctic. On the alpine tundra, where snow can fall on any day of the year, the growing season is reduced to about six weeks, hardly enough time for plants to grow from seed, reproduce, and make seeds. Consequently, few alpine plants are annuals. Most are perennials, plants that live for more than one year.

There is much to discover in each of the mountain ecosystems. The primary zones covered in this book include:

Foothills: 6,000 feet to 8,000 feet

Foothills vegetation forms a tapestry of inter-fingered plant communities. Grassy, flower-dotted meadows from the plains creep into the lower edges of this region. Gambel (or Scrub) Oak, Pinyon Pine, and Rocky Mountain Juniper form the backbone of the foothills ecosystem. Wildlife such as scrub jays, chipmunks and mule deer thrive on the seeds of these trees. In the higher foothills, Ponderosa Pines invade from the montane ecosystem above. Spring makes its appearance as

RICHARD BEIDLEMAN

Foothills

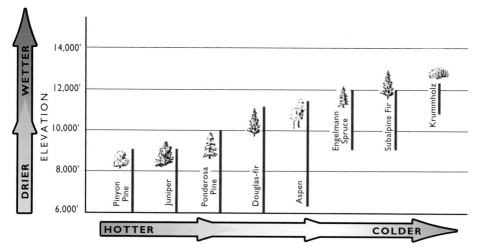

WETTER / DRIER

ELEVATION

14,000'
12,000'
10,000'
8,000'
6,000'

Pinyon Pine
Juniper
Ponderosa Pine
Douglas-fir
Aspen
Engelmann Spruce
Subalpine Fir
Krummholz

HOTTER → COLDER

These tree species are seen at higher elevations as you head farther south.

early as March, when the first delicate, lavender Pasqueflower pokes through the snow. Before long, other species, such as the white, starlike Sand Lily and the yellow-centered Easter Daisy, take the stage.

Montane: 8,000 feet to 9,500 feet

Spring comes later to these elevations. This region of Aspen, Ponderosa Pine, Douglas-fir, and Columbine epitomizes the splendor of the mountains for many people. Under proper conditions, wildflowers may carpet meadows in a single

Montane

color. Penstemons and lupines can paint the hillsides blue. Colorado Loco forms a sea of magenta. Balsamroot flowers fill valleys with yellow. Watchful hikers may spot black-crested Steller's jays, elk, and beaver. From central Colorado northward, great forests of Lodgepole Pine are common. These trees colonize areas burned by fire and produce dense stands.

ROCKY MOUNTAIN NATIONAL PARK

Subalpine

Subalpine: 9,500 feet to 11,500 feet

Dense forests of Engelmann Spruce and Subalpine Fir cover the upper reaches of the Southern Rocky Mountains. The trees' narrow, pointy shapes easily shed heavy snows that would break the branches of broader species.

Relatively few flowers grace the shady floors of these primeval forests. The sunflower-like heads of Heartleaf Arnica add a splash of yellow to the needles carpeting the forest floor. Meadows and streamsides sport a greater variety of wildflowers. Tall, purple Subalpine Larkspur and Monkshood can be found in moist meadows. On ridges, Limber Pines bend in the strong winds. Bristlecone Pines, among the Earth's oldest living things, may be more than 1,000 years old.

At the upper limits of the subalpine ecosystem, subalpine trees become stunted and twisted. There they are known as *krummholz*, a German term meaning crooked wood. Wind-blown ice and sand prune the limbs from the windward side of exposed trees. This weather blasting often permits growth of green branches only on the leeward side of the trunk. These malformed evergreens are called flag, or banner, trees.

Alpine: 11,500 feet and above

In their book *The Land Above the Trees,* Beatrice Willard and Ann Zwinger describe the alpine tundra as "a land of contrast and incredible intensity, where the sky is the size of forever and the flowers the size of a millisecond."

Intense cold and drying winds forbid the growth of trees, except for occasional dwarf willows. From afar, mountaintops look like forbidding fortresses of rock and snow. A closer examination reveals a stunning variety of plant communities. There are lush meadows of tiny flowers with the most intense colors imaginable. There are boulder fields that hide peeping pikas, small, grayish tan, short-eared relatives of rabbits. Atop the rocks, groundhog-like marmots sunbathe before their eight-month-long hibernation. Spring usually arrives in June to the rocky tundra meadows known as fellfields. One plant seen there is the cushion-shaped Moss Campion, an early bloomer soon covered with pink blossoms.

These ecosystems do not have perfect boundaries that fit precisely into the elevation levels just described. In New Mexico, timberline—the upper limit of tree growth—may reach to 12,200 feet elevation. In southern Wyoming, timberline is closer to 11,000 feet.

ROCKY MOUNTAIN NATIONAL PARK

Alpine

Another interesting quirk of the mountains is slope. The cooler, shadier north-facing slopes tend to be covered in thick evergreen forests. On the sunny, drier south-facing slopes, vegetation typically is more sparse. In the foothills and montane ecosystems, south-facing slopes often are covered with grasses, shrubs, Scrub Oaks, and widely spaced Ponderosa Pines. The north-facing slopes bear dense forests of Douglas-fir and Ponderosa Pine, along with Blue Spruce and White Fir.

The great variety of plant and animal life in the Southern Rockies provides much to discover. Learning how to identify and name some of the region's wildflowers is a great place to start your explorations. Please remember not to pick wildflowers. It harms nature's handiwork and may even be illegal. Be aware of all regulations in the area you visit, and carry a camera. Taking photographs or keeping a journal will provide memories that long outlive even the most colorful blooms.

How to Use This Guide

Anyone with an interest in America's Southern Rocky Mountains can use this guide as a tool for understanding the unique tapestry of plants found in the region. The book is designed to be used without any specialized knowledge, and technical terms have been eliminated, with a few necessary exceptions. There are hundreds of species of native flowering plants in this spectacular mountain region. This guide covers the more common and characteristic plants.

Included here are photographs and descriptions of 195 mountain plants. Plants are grouped according to flower color and divided into the following categories: **blue and purple, pink, red and orange, yellow, white,** and **green.**

Flower color is a convenient means of quickly grouping plants, but it is by no means a perfect system. Wildflowers, like all living things, are variable; no two individuals are exactly alike. The variation results from a combination of heredity (what were the parents like?) and environment (what are the conditions where it grows?). Just as there may be blond, black-, and red-haired people, a single species of plant may have a range of flower colors. Many plants with pink flowers, for instance, also have white-flowered forms. Grouping plants by color also is problematic because the difference between colors, such as blue and purple, is difficult to define. Some plants even have multicolored flowers. In this guide, plants are grouped according to the color that is most prevalent for the species. The best way to begin to identify a Southern Rockies wildflower is to go to the color section in this guide that matches the plant in question.

A written entry accompanies each plant photograph and includes the common and scientific names of the plant. Most high country plants have several common names, and a common name used in one region may apply elsewhere to a totally unrelated plant. The common names used in this book are selected to be the most appropriate through the Southern Rockies region. In some instances, additional common names are given in the Comments section of each entry.

Because of the confusion surrounding common names, the scientific name of the plant also is provided. These names, rendered in Latin, are a more stable and universal means of referring to a particular plant; the same scientific name usually is used worldwide. The scientific name consists of two words. The first word, the genus, is the name of a group of plants with similar general characteristics. The second part of the scientific name is the specific epithet, or specific name, which identifies the particular species of plant. Thus, there are many species of a single genus. Besides being consistent, scientific names show relationships by identifying species in the same genus. For example, *Mertensia ciliata*, the scientific name for Tall Chiming Bells, identifies it as the species *ciliata*, part of the larger genus *Mertensia*.

Most of the scientific names used in this book follow William Weber's *Colorado Flora: Eastern Slope*. However, all botanists do not agree on which scientific name is appropriate. In addition, the scientific names of some plants change over time. If a botanist discovers an older name for a plant, its scientific name reverts to the oldest recorded name. In addition, the names of some plant families have been changed. For example, the Sunflower family formerly was called Compositae. Then, it was decided that plant families should be named after a genus in that family. Consequently, the Sunflower family name was changed to Asteraceae because *Aster* is the name of a genus within that family. In recent years, botanists have decided to split up some plant families. Ladyslippers once were in the Orchid family, Orchidaceae. Some botanists have separated them into their own family, Cypripediaceae. In this book, some commonly used older scientific names appear in the Comments section, in parentheses directly following alternate common names.

In a few cases, the scientific name for a plant will have a third part, preceded by the word "variety," abbreviated "var.," or "subspecies," abbreviated "ssp." These are plants that differ slightly—but consistently—from other plants of the same species and often have distinct ranges.

Plants are grouped into families according to similarities in their structure and biology. The scientific name of a plant family always ends with the suffix "aceae," such as Asteraceae for the Aster family. With surprisingly little experience, many common plant families can be identified at first sight. Most people are already familiar with the unmistakable flowers of the Bean family (Fabaceae), which includes peas, beans, sweet peas, lupines, and locust flowers. Being able to determine the family of an unknown plant helps in field identification.

The main part of each entry contains a description of the plant. This description starts with general growth characteristics and identifying features. Leaves, flowers, and sometimes, fruits, are described. For many features such as plant height, leaf size, and flower dimensions, an approximate size or range of typical sizes is given in inches or feet. Unless otherwise stated, leaf measurements are for the leafy part of the plant only, and do not include the leaf stalk. The size ranges given are for typical plants. No size measurements are absolute, and diligent searching will reveal the odd, stunted individual or the overfertilized giant. But the measurements provided here will apply to most of the plants encountered in mountain habitats.

When identifying plants in the field, it helps to take a minute to study the plant, noting its general growth form, leaves, flowers, and any other distinguishing features. Look around for other plants of the same species. Maybe you will see better-developed or more fully blooming individuals. A small magnifying glass or hand lens with 10x magnification helps in seeing telltale hairs and flower parts.

The descriptions and photographs in this book are intended to be used together to identify a plant. There may be occasions when a plant does not exactly match an entry but clearly is a close relative. In many cases, this will be because the plant in question is of a different species but the same genus as the plant in the photograph. Sometimes, the Comments section mentions related species and how to identify them.

Although this guide keeps technical terms to a minimum, users will find knowledge of a few special terms is necessary. These terms, easy to learn and useful for all plant identification, are discussed below. A complete list of terms is included in the glossary at the back of this book.

Many of the plants listed in this book are perennial, that is, parts of the plant live anywhere from a few years to more than a century. Familiar examples of perennial plants include tulips, raspberries, and oak trees. Perennial plants can be divided into two types: woody plants such as trees and shrubs, and herbaceous plants that die back to ground level each year, with only the underground parts overwintering. Most Southern Rocky Mountain plants are herbaceous perennials; only a small percentage of this high country flora is composed of woody plants. In addition to perennials, herbaceous plants may be classified as annuals, which germinate, flower, produce seeds, and die within a year, or biennials, which take two years to produce seeds before dying.

It often is easy to determine whether a plant is perennial since parts of the previous year's growth may be visible. Perennial plants generally have well-developed underground parts such as bulbs or large tuberous roots, while annual plants typically have a small system of fibrous roots. Plants discussed in this book are perennial unless stated otherwise, and all plants in the book are herbaceous unless they are specifically listed as woody.

Each plant description provides the diagnostic features needed for identification, including discussion of overall appearance, leaves, and flowers. Sometimes, features such as fragrant leaves or colored or milky sap will be mentioned. These can be determined by gently squeezing and then smelling a leaf, and by slightly tearing the tip of a leaf and noting the sap color. Some plants have winged parts, thin strips of tissue attached edgewise along a stem, branch, or other part.

Another feature often useful in plant identification is the presence of hairs on leaves, stems, or flower parts. Some plants are always hairless, some are always hairy, and individual plants within some species may range from hairless to hairy. The size, abundance, and type of hairs are often useful for identification purposes. In this guide, the discussion for each plant includes whether the plant is hairy or smooth—if this is a useful feature for identification. If the hairiness is not mentioned, it means that the plant can be smooth or hairy, or that the hairs are small, sparse, and easily overlooked.

Leaves are important identifying features of wildflowers. To describe small differences precisely, botanists use dozens of technical terms for the shapes, textures, surfaces, margins, parts, and attachments of leaves. This book avoids such terms. Leaf shapes are described using common language such as "long and narrow" or "broadly oval."

Important leaf features to note include arrangement of the leaves on the stem (opposite each other, alternating along the stem, or whorled, that is, several leaves from one point), and the leaf tip (pointed or blunt), leaf base (tapering, rounded, heart-shaped, or clasping the stem), leaf edges (smooth, toothed, wavy, or lobed), leaf texture (thick, leathery, waxy, thin, or brittle), and whether the leaves are on stalks or stalkless. Many plants produce basal leaves; these leaves originate directly from the underground parts of the plant and are not attached to the stems. Sometimes, the shape of the basal leaves may differ from the stem leaves or the basal leaves may have different stalks.

Any leaves not identified as compound are simple leaves (See Figure 1A). Simple leaves have a single, leaflike blade above each bud. This blade may be lobed or unlobed, but it is clearly a single leaf. Compound leaves are divided into two or more distinct segments called leaflets, with each segment often looking

Figure 1. Variations of leaf arrangement (A), shape (B), and margin (C)

A. Leaf Arrangement

Alternate: one leaf
to a node

Opposite: two leaves
to a node

Whorled: three or more
leaves to a node

Basal rosette

Simple

Pinnately compound leaves: leaflets
arranged on both sides of the leaf stalk

Palmately compound leaves: leaflets
spreading like fingers from the
palm of the hand

B. Leaf Shape

Needlelike

Linear

Lance-shaped

Oblong

Elliptical

Round

Egg-shaped

Inversely lance-shaped

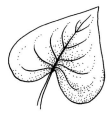

Heart-shaped

Spatula-shaped

Wedge-shaped

Triangular

C. Leaf Margin

Entire   Toothed   Wavy

Lobed   Doubly toothed   Cleft

like a separate leaf. The only sure way to identify a compound leaf is to look for buds. If there are several leaflike segments above a single bud, you are dealing with a compound leaf. This can be tricky, but is important to master since many plant groups can be quickly determined by this feature. Leaflets of compound leaves can be arranged featherlike along a stalklike axis, or originate from a common point like the fingers on a hand, or even be doubly or triply compound, with each segment divided once or twice again into further series of leaflike segments. In all cases, however, the leaflets of compound leaves are arranged in the same plane.

Features related to leaves are bracts. These are reduced, leaflike structures or scales, and often are associated with flowers. Sometimes, bracts are like miniature versions of the plant's leaves. Sometimes, they are just little pointed or rounded green scales and sometimes they are totally different in size and shape from the leaves. Bracts may be green and leaflike in texture, thin and papery, or sometimes, even colored like flower petals. On some plants, there are two specialized bractlike structures called stipules at the base of the leaf stalk. These may be large and showy, or tiny and scalelike, or they may fall off soon after the leaf emerges from the bud.

Flowers are the most complicated parts of a plant. They come in an array of shapes, sizes, and colors. Flower descriptions in this guide are intended to help in identification, so only prominent or distinctive flower characteristics are discussed. Lack of discussion of a particular feature does not mean it is lacking for that species, but only that it is not a useful characteristic for identification.

Flowers have one main function—to facilitate pollination of the female flower parts and development of the seeds and fruits. Flowers that are insect pollinated often have showy or fragrant parts to attract suitable pollinators. On the other hand, flowers that are wind pollinated, such as many trees and grasses, have very reduced flowers suited to launching and capturing wind-blown pollen without the need for showy or fragrant parts. **Flowers of plants such as grasses are highly modified and are not discussed in detail in this book.**

A diagram of a generalized flower is given in Figure 2. Most flowers have an outer series of flower parts, called sepals, surrounding the base of the flower. Sepals often are green and can be inconspicuous, but they also can be showy and colored. The sepals together form the calyx. The calyx may be composed of separate sepals, or the sepals may be joined or fused into a tube or cuplike calyx. If the sepals are fused, they often are represented by teeth or points around the top of the calyx.

Inside the calyx of most flowers is a series of usually showy parts called petals. These are what we first see when we view the average flower. The petals come in a variety of shapes, sizes, and colors, and depending on the kind of plant, there

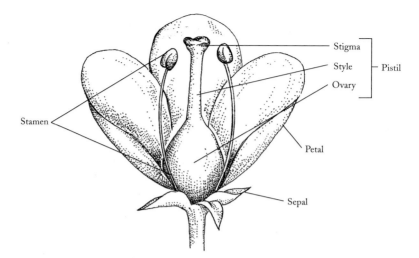

Figure 2. Typical flower in cross section

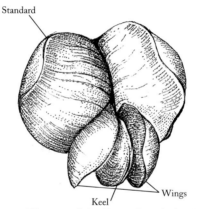

Figure 3. Flower of the Bean family (Fabaceae)

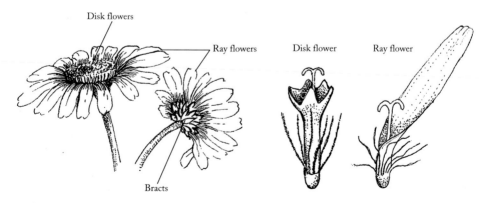

Figure 4. Flowers of the Sunflower family (Asteraceae)

may be no petals or three to six or more per flower. The petals may be separate from each other or partially or wholly fused together into a cuplike, tubular, or irregular shape. The petals together, whether fused or separate, form the corolla. Some flowers have no corolla and in some plants, the sepals and petals are identical and are called tepals.

Within the flower, pollen is produced by the stamens. There may be one to more than 100 stamens per flower. Stamens typically are long, thin filaments with clublike or elongate appendages at the tip. The seed-producing part of the flower is called the pistil. This consists of the usually swollen ovary where the seeds develop, above which is a usually long, tubelike style with a blunt, divided, or elongate stigma at the tip that serves as a pollen receptor. In some flowers, the style is absent. While most flowers have both male (stamen) and female (pistil) parts, some plants have separate male and female flowers and in some species, male and female flowers are on separate plants.

The arrangement of flowers on a plant also is useful for identification purposes. Again, botanists use many specialized terms to describe the arrangement of flowers on a plant. Because these terms are confusing and can be hard to determine, they are avoided here. Flower arrangements are described in general terms such as "open clusters" or "narrow elongate spikes."

Two families of flowers, both well represented in the Southern Rockies, have specialized flower structures that deserve comment. Most plants in the Bean family (Fabaceae) have a calyx surrounding five petals that are developed into a specialized form. The upper petal, called the standard, is erect, spreading, and usually the largest. Below this are two protruding side petals, called wings, closely surrounding the keel, which is actually created by the fusion of the two lowest petals. A typical Bean family flower is shown in Figure 3.

Asters, goldenrods, daisies, dandelions, and other plants in the Aster family (Asteraceae) have an unusual flower arrangement. What appears at first glance to be a single flower is actually a head composed of a few to several hundred small flowers. This head of flowers usually is surrounded at the base by a series of bracts. The calyx is absent or reduced to bristles, scales, or hairs. Two kinds of flowers are produced: disk flowers and ray flowers (Figure 4), as described below.

The corollas of ray flowers have a single, usually brightly colored strap that looks like the petal of a conventional flower. Disk flowers have small, tubular corollas, usually with five lobes. Depending on the species, each flower head may be all disk flowers, all ray flowers, or a combination of the two. When both are present, there usually is a central circle or cone of disk flowers surrounded by one or more series of ray flowers, the whole creating the appearance of a single typical flower although there may be more than 100 flowers present. A typical Aster family flower head is diagrammed in Figure 4.

Following the **Description** of each plant is a section titled **Habitat/Range.** This provides a summary of the typical Southern Rocky Mountain habitats for the plant and a general range where the plant grows within the region. These habitat statements apply only to the Southern Rockies. Plants that grow at 13,000 feet in Colorado may be found at 435 feet elevation in Alaska. Plants that grow along streams in the West may be found in meadows in the East.

The **Habitat/Range** section also includes comments about the relative abundance of plants, using terms such as "common," "occasional," and "rare." These are general terms to give the user an idea of the relative rarity of each species, but are intended merely as rangewide guides. Species described as common throughout the Southern Rockies may be rare or absent in a particular area, and rare species may be locally abundant in some areas.

Most entries also have a section called **Comments**. This provides information such as discussions of closely related species, historical uses for the plant, and other notes of interest. Several plants in this book are listed as having been eaten or used as medicine. This information is presented for historical perspective only and, in many cases, is based on literature reports. Because of the uncertainties of plant identification and the lack of information about the accuracy of early reports, these plants should not be eaten or used medicinally since many edible plants have poisonous counterparts.

Blue and Purple Flowers

This section includes flowers ranging from pale blue to deep indigo and from lavender to violet. Since purple flowers grade into pink flowers, readers looking for purple flowers should check the pink section as well.

LORAINE YEATTS

Alpine Fleabane

ALPINE FLEABANE
Erigeron simplex
Aster family (Asteraceae)

Description: A single flower head, 1" wide, is borne on each 1–10" stalk. The 50–125 ray flowers on each head are blue, purple, or pink. The bracts have white or red woolly hairs. The entire, primarily basal leaves are 3½" long, with smaller leaves on the stem.

Mid- to late summer.

Habitat/Range: Common in moist subalpine and alpine meadows from Montana south to Arizona and New Mexico.

Comments: This flower looks much like the Blackheaded Daisy (*E. melanocephalus);* however, the bracts of the Blackheaded Daisy have dark purple to black hairs.

ASPEN DAISY
Erigeron speciosus
Aster family (Asteraceae)

Description: Heads are 1–2" across with 1–11 heads per stem. Numerous (70–150) blue, lavender, or light pink, narrow ray flowers surround a yellow center. Branching stems 6–30" tall bear 3-veined leaves. The stem leaves are slightly shorter than the 3–6" long basal leaves. Leaves are lance-shaped and only have hairs along the edges.

Midsummer.

Habitat/Range: Found in fields and sunny forests in the foothills, montane, and subalpine ecosystems from Canada to New Mexico.

Comments: Also known as Showy Daisy. Often confused with asters, erigerons usually have fewer heads per stalk and narrower, more numerous ray flowers. Also, they bloom earlier than the asters. The bracts around the heads of erigerons usually are about the same length and are aligned in one or two rows.

H. WAYNE PHILLIPS

Aspen Daisy

SMOOTH ASTER
Aster laevis var. *geyeri*
Aster family (Asteraceae)

Description: The petals of these daisylike flowers are blue to violet around a yellow center. Flower heads are ½–1" across with 1 to many heads per stem. The foliage is hairless, hence its common name. A whitish coating covers the 2–7¾" long leaves. The lower leaves have short, winged stalks and are longer than the unstalked upper leaves that clasp the stems. The thick leaves are slightly toothed, much longer than wide, and have a pointed tip. The stems are from 1' to more than 3' tall.

Late summer to fall.

Habitat/Range: Common in both dry and moist forests of the foothills and montane ecosystems. It blooms from the Rocky Mountains to the Atlantic Ocean.

Comments: A dye can be made from this aster's foliage. Colors range from yellowish green to orange.

Smooth Aster

Alpine Forget-Me-Not

ALPINE FORGET-ME-NOT
Eritrichum aretioides
Borage family (Boraginaceae)

Description: These brilliant blue flowers with yellow centers are only ¼" across. The sweet-smelling blossoms occasionally are white. Flowers are funnel-shaped with 5 lobes. Leaves and stems of this cushion plant are covered with silvery hairs. The leaves are thick and less than ½" long. The plants typically are under 4" tall.

Early to midsummer.

Habitat/Range: Found in the gravelly soil of windy alpine fellfields. In the United States, they range from Montana to New Mexico.

Comments: This plant is similar to Howard's Alpine Forget-Me-Not found in Montana and northern Wyoming. *E. howardii*, however, has narrower, longer leaves covered with short hairs and darker blue flowers and is found on dry ridges below timberline.

LORAINE YEATTS

Lanceleaf Chiming Bells

LANCELEAF CHIMING BELLS
Mertensia lanceolata
Borage family (Boraginaceae)

Description: This plant's dangling, bell-shaped blue flowers are similar to those of Tall Chiming Bells. The inner surface of the 5-lobed flower has a ring of short hairs. Leaves are alternate, less than 1¼" wide, and have only a single prominent vein. Upper leaf surfaces are covered with short, fine hairs. The undersides of the leaves are smooth. Stems are 10–15" tall.

Spring to early summer.

Habitat/Range: Common in meadows of the foothills and montane ecosystems from Canada to New Mexico. Some botanists classify a shorter (under 2" tall), alpine version of this plant as *M. viridis*.

Comments: Another relative of this plant grows exclusively on the alpine tundra of Pikes Peak near Colorado Springs, Colorado. The flowers of this plant, Alpine Chiming Bells *(M. alpina)*, are wider than long. Leafy Bluebells *(M. oblongifolia)*, found from Montana to northwestern Colorado, lacks a ring of hairs inside the blossom. The upper leaf surface of Utah Mertensia *(M. fusiformis)*, found in western Colorado and Utah, has hairs that point toward the edge of the leaf.

TALL CHIMING BELLS
Mertensia ciliata
Borage family (Boraginaceae)

Description: This plant's common name describes the bell-shaped flowers dangling from tall, leafy stems. The flower buds typically are pink, opening into sky blue, tubular flowers. The corolla has 5 lobes and is more than 3⅜" long. Smooth, alternate leaves have several prominent veins. The bluish green leaves may be up to 2⅜" wide. This branching plant grows 1–4' tall.

Early to late summer.

Habitat/Range: Forms lush, dense stands in boggy meadows and along shaded subalpine streams. May also be found in alpine areas and at lower elevations. It is seen throughout the Rockies from Montana to New Mexico.

Comments: Also called Mountain Bluebells. Deer, elk, bear, and pikas eat this plant.

ROCKY MOUNTAIN NATIONAL PARK

Tall Chiming Bells

Mountain Harebell

MOUNTAIN HAREBELL
Campanula rotundifolia
Bellflower family (Campanulaceae)

Description: These delicate "bluebells of Scotland" hang daintily from slender stalks. The lavender blue flowers are ½–¾" long with a similar width. Several blossoms dangle from each 4–31" stem. The specific name *rotundifolia* describes the round, toothed basal leaves. The alternate, linear stem leaves are 1–3" long.

Early to late summer.

Habitat/Range: Common in both dry and moist sites from the foothills to the alpine tundra. Its wide range extends from Alaska to California and New Mexico. This circumboreal plant also is found in Eurasia.

Comments: The generic name *Campanula* means "small bell."

Parry Harebell

PARRY HAREBELL
Campanula parryi
Bellflower family (Campanulaceae)

Description: Violet, bell-shaped flowers stand erect on the slender stalks of this plant. The ½" long blossoms have 5 pointed lobes, 5 stamens, and a 3-lobed stigma. There usually is only 1 flower on each stalk. Stems are 4–12" tall with narrow leaves. The lower stem leaves are fringed with white hairs. Leaves are entire and 1–2" long.

Midsummer.

Habitat/Range: Found in aspen groves and moist meadows in the montane to lower alpine ecosystems from Montana to New Mexico.

Comments: The blue flowers of Alpine Harebell *(C. uniflora)* are borne on stalks under 4" tall. Its leaves lack obvious hairs.

SPIDERWORT
Tradescantia occidentalis
Spiderwort family (Commelinaceae)

Description: Loose clusters of deep blue, purple, or rose-colored flowers grow on smooth, weedy-looking stems. The blossoms have 3 petals; 6 hairy stamens bear bright yellow pollen at their tips. Green sepals and flower stalks usually bear sticky hairs. Below the stalks are 2–3 leafy bracts. Each 1–1½" wide flower blooms for only one day. The bases of the alternate, grasslike leaves form a sheath around the stem. This plant grows 6–24" tall.

Late spring to midsummer.

Habitat/Range: Found in fields, on gravelly hillsides, and along trails in the foothills ecosystem from Montana to New Mexico.

Comments: A similar species, Western Dayflower *(Commelina dianthifolia)*, grows from central Colorado to Mexico and has blue flowers above a folded bract with a long, pointy tip.

Spiderwort

Mountain Lupine

MOUNTAIN LUPINE
Lupinus argenteus
Bean family (Fabaceae)

Description: Tall, showy clusters of blue or pink, pea-like flowers make this plant eye catching. Flowers are ½" long, 2-lipped, and may be partially white. The alternate, palmately compound leaves have 5–9 leaflets. The leaves and stems are covered with gray hairs, hence the name *argenteus*, which means "silvery." Stems are up to 30" tall. The beanlike seedpods are hairy and up to 1" long.

Mid- to late summer.

Habitat/Range: Common in meadows and forest edges of the foothills, montane, and subalpine ecosystems.

Comments: Also called Silvery or Common Lupine. May be confused with Nebraska Lupine *(L. plattensis)*, which has blue flowers that are more than ½" long and also have a purple spot on the standard. A white-flowered subspecies, *(L. Ingratus),* is common in the eastern foothills of Colorado's Front Range.

ROCKY MOUNTAIN NATIONAL PARK

Fringed Gentian

FRINGED GENTIAN
Gentianopsis thermalis
Gentian family (Gentianaceae)

Description: As the name suggests, the 4 lobes of this bright blue to purple flower are fringed. A single tubular blossom rests upon each slender stalk. The 1–2" long flowers have 4 pointed sepals and a 2-parted stigma. This annual plant has opposite leaves and grows to 16" tall.

Mid- to late summer.

Habitat/Range: Found in sunny, moist areas of the montane, subalpine, and alpine ecosystems from Canada to New Mexico.

Comments: This plant was given its species name, *thermalis*, because it grows near Yellowstone National Park's hot springs. It may be confused with the lighter-colored, sweet-smelling flowers of Fragrant Gentian *(G. barbellata).*

PARRY GENTIAN
Pneumonanthe parryi
Gentian family (Gentianaceae)

Description: These gobletlike flowers have a true blue color with green bands. There are pleats between the 5 lobes of 1–1½" long blossoms. The stems may have 1 to several flowers and may be up to 15" tall. The smooth, oval leaves are opposite and entire.

Mid- to late summer.

Habitat/Range: Graces meadows of the subalpine ecosystem from Wyoming to New Mexico.

Comments: Also called Mountain, Blue, or Bottle Gentian. These and several other gentian flowers close up in cloudy or rainy weather. The Alpine Moss Gentian *(Chondrophylla prostrata)* has light blue or purple flowers that are less than 1" long.

Parry Gentian

PLEATED GENTIAN
Pneumonanthe affinis
Gentian family (Gentianaceae)

Description: These blue to indigo flowers are similar to the Parry Gentian *(P. parryi)*, but lack the green bands. The 5-lobed blossoms are pleated and ¾"–1⅛" long. There are several flowers on the stems, which grow to 15" in height and curve at the base. Leaves are opposite and entire.

Mid- to late summer.

Habitat/Range: This common flower blooms in meadows of the foothills and montane ecosystems from Canada to Arizona.

Comments: Also called Prairie Gentian or Bottle Gentian *(Gentiana affinis)*. The roots of several species of gentians were used as a stomach tonic by Native Americans and early settlers.

Pleated Gentian

Star Gentian

STAR GENTIAN
Swertia perennis
Gentian family (Gentianaceae)

Description: These clustered, star-shaped flowers typically are blue to purple, but occasionally white. Each of the 4–5 lobes have 2 fringed glands at the base. The stamens protrude from the ¾" wide flowers. The smooth leaves are chiefly basal and up to 6" long. The opposite stem leaves are much smaller. These perennial plants grow from rhizomes to heights of 16".

Midsummer to early fall.

Habitat/Range: Found in open, wet areas of the montane, subalpine, and alpine ecosystems. This circumboreal plant occurs in North America from Alaska to New Mexico.

Comments: This species is also called Felwort (from *fel,* "rock," and *wort,* "plant"). The genus was named for a sixteenth-century Dutch author and gardener Emanuel Sweert.

Purple Fringe

PURPLE FRINGE
Phacelia sericea
Waterleaf family (Hydrophyllaceae)

Description: This plant's fringed look comes from the long stamens that protrude from tight clusters of purple flowers. The bell-shaped blossoms are ¼" long with 5 rounded lobes. The hairy leaves are 1–4" long and are pinnately divided into lobes. Stems are 4–12" tall and are often branched at the base.

Early to late summer.

Habitat/Range: This common plant grows well in disturbed soils along roads and on gravelly slopes. It is found in the montane, subalpine, and alpine ecosystems from Alaska to Colorado.

Comments: Also called Silky Phacelia and Purple Pincushion. The specific name *sericea* means "silky," referring to the soft hairs on the foliage. A similar species, *P. bakeri*, has sticky hairs and flower clusters that start out coiled like a fiddlehead.

MOUNTAIN BLUE-EYED GRASS
Sisyrinchium montanum
Iris family (Iridaceace)

Description: Despite its name and the shape of its leaves, this plant is not a grass. The blue, starlike flowers are less than ¾" across and typically have a yellow center. The 3 petals and 3 sepals look exactly alike. The slender stems are 5–12" tall. The fruits are small, round berries.

Late spring to midsummer.

Habitat/Range: Common in grassy areas of the foothills, montane, and subalpine ecosystems. This species is found from Canada to New Mexico.

Comments: *Sisyrinchium* means "swine snout"; it is named for a Greek plant whose roots were favored by pigs.

Mountain Blue-Eyed Grass

MOUNTAIN IRIS
Iris missouriensis
Iris family (Iridaceace)

Description: This bluish purple wild iris looks much like its garden relatives. Flowers are 3" across. The 3 yellow-streaked sepals bend downward; the 3 petals stick up, as do the 3 petal-like style branches that hide the stamens. The leafless flower stalk is surrounded by clumps of swordlike leaves that are 8–20" long, smooth, entire, and have parallel veins. The fruit is a 3-parted capsule.

Late spring to midsummer.

Habitat/Range: Found in wet meadows and along streams in the foothills, montane, and subalpine ecosystems. Mountain Iris is seen from British Columbia and North Dakota south to California and New Mexico.

Comments: Several western Native American nations soaked the roots in animal bile and used the mixture on arrows as poison. Orris root, a fixative used in potpourris and perfumes, comes from irises.

Mountain Iris

BRITTON SKULLCAP
Scutellaria brittonii
Mint family (Lamiaceae)

Description: A ridge on top of these deep blue to purple, paired flowers helps distinguish skullcaps from other mints. The flowers are 1" long and have upper and lower lips. Blossoms are attached where the opposite leaves meet the square, 4–12" stem. The leaves are entire and the foliage may be smooth or covered with sticky hairs.

Late spring to midsummer.

Habitat/Range: Grows on dry hillsides in the foothills and montane ecosystems from Wyoming to New Mexico.

Comments: Between the eighteenth and the early twentieth centuries, skullcap was made into a medicine believed to alleviate tremors and convulsions; one species was used to treat rabies.

Britton Skullcap

Blue Flax

BLUE FLAX
Adenolinum lewisii
Flax family (Linaceae)

Description: Delicate sky blue flowers rest on slender stalks that sway in mountain breezes. The 5 petals open in the morning and may fall off the same afternoon. The center of the blossom is yellow, ¾–1½" wide, with 5 stamens and a 5-parted stigma. Narrow, alternate leaves are ½–1¼" long. The tough stems may be up to 32" tall. The round seedpods are the size of a small pea.

Spring to late summer.

Habitat/Range: Sunny meadows in the foothills and montane ecosystems from Alaska to Mexico.

Comments: Also known as *Linus lewisii.* Members of the Lewis and Clark Expedition collected this plant on their exploration of the Louisiana Purchase. Its specific name honors Captain Meriwether Lewis.

ALPINE PHLOX
Phlox sibirica ssp. *pulvinata*
Phlox family (Polemoniaceae)

Description: Five white to light blue or pink petals unite to form a funnel-shaped tube at the base of these flowers. The blossoms, about ¼–½" long, are borne singly at the top of a short stem. The crowded, entire leaves are less than ⅜" long. The sticky, hairy foliage forms cushionlike mats.

Midsummer.

Habitat/Range: Common in rocky alpine meadows. Also found in subalpine areas from Montana to New Mexico.

Comments: The specific name *pulvinata* means "cushionlike," hence its other common name, Cushion Phlox. Many-Flowered Phlox *(P. multiflora)* has longer, smooth leaves and longer flowers. Tufted Phlox *(P. condensata)* has shorter leaves and flowers.

Alpine Phlox

Sky Pilot

SKY PILOT
Polemonium viscosum
Phlox family (Polemoniaceae)

Description: This plant features bright blue, lavender, or occasionally white, skunky-smelling flowers ½–¾" long with 5 rounded lobes. The 5 stamens, tipped with orange pollen, are hard to miss. The funnel-shaped blossoms are clustered at the top of a hairy, sticky stem. The hairy sepals are almost as long as the fused flower tube. The leaves are pinnately divided, up to 6" long, and chiefly basal. This plant usually grows from 3–16" tall.

Early to late summer.

Habitat/Range: Seen on rocky alpine slopes and disturbed ground from Canada to New Mexico. Sky Pilot flourishes in "gopher gardens," meadows full of gopher mounds and burrows.

Comments: Also called Skunkweed. The odor of Sky Pilot may vary, depending on the race or population of flowers.

Subalpine Jacob's Ladder

SUBALPINE JACOB'S LADDER
Polemonium pulcherrimum ssp. *delicatum*
Phlox family (Polemoniaceae)

Description: The lobes of this *Polemonium* are longer than the flower tube. Colors range from violet to sky blue, with occasional clusters of white or pink blossoms. The flowers are ¼–½" long in small clusters. The 5 sepals are pointed and hairy. Five stamens surround a 3-parted stigma. The pinnately compound leaves resemble tiny ladders and are mostly basal. The sprawling stems are under 10" tall and woolly.

Early to late summer.

Habitat/Range: Often found in the shade of evergreens in the subalpine ecosystem, it also grows at timberline and on the alpine tundra from Wyoming to New Mexico.

Comments: Like many other *polemoniums*, this flower has a strong, skunky smell.

WESTERN JACOB'S LADDER
Polemonium caeruleum ssp. *amygdalinum*
Phlox family (Polemoniaceae)

Description: The specific name *caeruleum* refers to this flower's blue color. The blossoms are longer than wide and like those of other *polemoniums* have 5 petals, 5 sepals, and 5 stamens. The leaflets of the pinnately compound leaves are mostly without hairs. Upper leaves are much smaller than lower leaves, which may be up to 16" long. The stalk is unbranched and may be 20" tall.

Early to late summer.

Habitat/Range: Relatively uncommon, this species is found in swampy areas and open forests of the montane and subalpine ecosystems from Canada to Colorado.

Comments: The Latin name *amygdalinum* means "almond odor," although some people think the flowers smell skunky.

LEANNE BENTON

Western Jacob's Ladder

ALPINE COLUMBINE
Aquilegia saximontana
Buttercup family (Ranunculaceae)

Description: These nodding flowers look much like those of their larger cousin, the Colorado Columbine. The blossoms are less than 1" across with short, curved spurs. Leaves are primarily basal and have 3 leaflets with rounded lobes. Stems usually are less than 4" tall.

Midsummer.

Habitat/Range: This rare plant may be found hiding under the edges of boulders or on rocky slopes in the subalpine and alpine ecosystems. It is found only in Colorado.

Comments: *A. saximontana* also is called Dwarf Columbine. A similar species, Jones's Columbine *(A. jonesii)*, has all-blue flowers and can be found from Canada to Wyoming. Some botanists place this species in the Hellebore family (Helleboraceae).

ROCKY MOUNTAIN NATIONAL PARK

Alpine Columbine

American Pasqueflower

AMERICAN PASQUEFLOWER
Pulsatilla patens ssp. *multifida*
Buttercup family (Ranunculaceae)

Description: This dainty lavender flower is one of the first to open in the spring. The cup-shaped blossom is 1–2" across with 5–7 sepals. The delicately colored sepals have soft hairs on the outer surface. Many stamens add a touch of yellow to the center of the flower. The hairy flower stem bears 1 blossom with leaves to protect the bud. Additional lobed leaves appear at the plant's base once blooming is completed. The stem may grow to 16". The numerous seeds bear feathery tails.

Early spring to early summer.

Habitat/Range: Meadows and open forests in the foothills, montane, and subalpine ecosystems from Alaska to Texas.

Comments: An alternate common name is Anemone, based on the Greek word for "wind." Native Americans of the prairies called it Red-Calf-Flower. *Pasque* is French for "Easter."

Colorado Columbine

COLORADO COLUMBINE
Aquilegia coerulea
Buttercup family (Ranunculaceae)

Description: Colorado's state flower has 5 blue to lavender sepals and 5 funnel-shaped white petals with narrow blue spurs. The blossoms are 2–3" across with numerous yellow stamens protruding from the center of the flower. The compound leaves have deep, rounded lobes. Stems may be 8–24" tall.

Midsummer.

Habitat/Range: Moist soils, aspen groves, and rocky meadows of the foothills, montane, subalpine, and alpine ecosystems. Extends from Montana to New Mexico.

Comments: Also called Blue Columbine. Other varieties occasionally may be seen, including a white-flowered form and one that is blue and spurless. Some botanists place this species in the Hellebore family (Helleboraceae).

MONKSHOOD
Aconitum columbianum
Buttercup family (Ranunculaceae)

Description: The deep purplish blue upper sepal of this blossom forms a hood that covers most of the other flower parts. The 5 sepals occasionally may be white or greenish white. The ⅝"–1¼" long flowers are borne on stalks along the stem, which may be more than 4' tall. The leaves are alternate, 2–7" across, and have toothed lobes.

Early to late summer.

Habitat/Range: Found along streams and in wet meadows primarily in the montane and subalpine ecosystems from Canada to New Mexico.

Comments: Similar in appearance to larkspurs, Monkshood lacks the spurred sepal. The generic name *Aconitum* may be loosely translated as "unconquerable poison." All parts of this plant are poisonous. Some botanists place this species in the Hellebore family (Helleboraceae).

Monkshood

NELSON LARKSPUR
Delphinium nuttallium
Buttercup family (Ranunculaceae)

Description: An open cluster of 4–10 bright purplish blue flowers arises from a stalk that lacks sticky hairs. The 5 sepals form spurred flowers about 1" across and ½–¾" long. Four tiny petals are blue or white with blue markings. The leaves are 3" wide and are palmately divided into slender lobes. Stem leaves are alternate and few. The stems usually are single and unbranched. Plants grow to 6–20" in height from a tuberlike root.

Spring to midsummer.

Habitat/Range: Dry, sunny hillsides and beneath Ponderosa Pines in the foothills and montane ecosystems from Canada to Colorado.

Comments: Similar species include the taller Mountain Larkspur *(D. ramosum)*, which has small flowers and several stems. Some botanists place this species in the Hellebore family (Helleboraceae).

Nelson Larkspur

Rock Clematis

ROCK CLEMATIS
Atragene occidentalis
Buttercup family (Ranunculaceae)

Description: This plant's 4 lavender-blue "petals" actually are sepals. The flowers are ¾–2" long and arise singly from the point where the leaves attach to the stem. The opposite, compound leaves have 3 entire to barely toothed leaflets. The long stems are vines that climb up bushes and trees. The showy clumps of seeds have feathery tails.

Late spring to midsummer.

Habitat/Range: Woods and forest edges in the foothills, montane, and subalpine ecosystems from Canada to Colorado.

Comments: Also called Blue Clematis *(Clematis occidentalis)*. Two related plants have purple, leathery flowers. Sugarbowls *(Coriflora hirsutissima)* has compound leaves divided into narrow segments and Scott Clematis *(Coriflora scottii)* has ovate, entire leaflets. The petal-like sepals are a common characteristic of buttercups.

Subalpine Larkspur

SUBALPINE LARKSPUR
Delphinium barbeyi
Buttercup family (Ranunculaceae)

Description: Like many other members of this family, larkspurs have colorful, showy sepals. There are 5 dark purple sepals; the top one bears a ⅜" spur. The small petals are edged with white. The flowers are borne in a cluster atop a stem 3–6' tall. Leaves are palmately divided into 5–7 toothed lobes. The large, smooth leaves are found primarily on the stem, with few basal leaves. Several sticky, hairy stems arise from 1 rootstock.

Midsummer.

Habitat/Range: Seen on stream banks and in wet areas and forest openings in the subalpine and alpine ecosystems. Found in Utah, Colorado, New Mexico, and Arizona.

Comments: Some botanists place this species in the Hellebore family (Helleboraceae).

DWARF LOUSEWORT
Pedicularis centranthera
Figwort Family (Scrophulariaceae)

Description: The closely crowded flowers of dwarf lousewort are on stems that are shorter than the surrounding leaves. The petals are near-ly white at the base, becoming pale orchid to purple near the helmet-shaped tip. The leaves have many pinnately arranged segments, curled and crinkly, with white-tipped teeth. This is a low-growing herb, about 6" tall.

Spring to early summer.

Habitat/Range: Found in Pinyon-Juniper and Ponderosa Pine woodlands of the foothills and montane ecosystems of Colorado, Utah, and New Mexico.

Comments: *Pedicularis* is Latin for "louse." It was once thought that livestock which ate these plants would become infested with lice. Herb-alists use some species of lousewort as sedatives and muscle relaxants.—*H. Wayne Phillips*

Dwarf Lousewort

LORAINE YEATTS

Low Penstemon

LOW PENSTEMON
Penstemon virens
Snapdragon family (Scrophulariaceae)

Description: These dainty, royal blue to violet, tubular flowers have 2 lobes on top and 3 below. The ⅜–¾" long blossoms have sticky hairs on the outside. One of the 5 stamens is sterile and hairy. Flowers are in clusters atop a 4–14" stem. The shiny leaves are opposite, with upper leaves clasping the stem. The erect stems grow in clumps.

Late spring to midsummer.

Habitat/Range: Masses of these blue flowers color dry hillsides from the foothills through the subalpine ecosystems in Wyoming and Colorado.

Comments: Also called Blue Mist or Greenleaf Penstemon. *Penstemon* means "five stamens."

LORAINE YEATTS

Mountain Beardtongue

MOUNTAIN BEARDTONGUE
Penstemon glaber
Snapdragon family (Scrophulariaceae)

Description: Bright blue flowers are tightly clustered on one side of the stem. The blossoms have a 2-lobed upper lip and 3-lobed lower lip. Flowers are ¾–1¼" long. The 5th, sterile, stamen is smooth or hairy only on the tip. The opposite leaves are green, or sometimes bluish. The stems are stout, erect, and may be up to 31" tall and grouped in clumps.

Early to late summer.

Habitat/Range: Common along roadsides and slopes in the foothills, montane, and subalpine ecosystems from Wyoming to New Mexico.

Comments: Also called Pikes Peak Penstemon. This species was first collected on Pikes Peak in 1820 by Edwin James, the first documented white man to climb the peak. The name "beardtongue" refers to the sterile stamen's hairy tip.

ROCKY MOUNTAIN NATIONAL PARK

Tall One-Side Penstemon

TALL ONE-SIDE PENSTEMON
Penstemon virgatus ssp. *asa-grayi*
Snapdragon family (Scrophulariaceae)

Description: As the name implies, these flowers are clustered on one side of the stem. The outside of each blossom is blue and the inside is pinkish. The flowers are ⅝–1" long, tubular, and they flare out abruptly from the base. The 5th, sterile, stamen has no, or few, hairs. The opposite, narrow leaves lack the heavy white coating common to some penstemons. The stout stem may be up to 16" tall.

Midsummer.

Habitat/Range: Common on hills and mesas in the foothills and montane ecosystems from Wyoming to New Mexico.

Comments: This subspecies is named in honor of Asa Gray, curator of the botanical garden at Harvard University in the mid-nineteenth century. This plant is similar to Bearded Sidebells Penstemon *(P. secundiflorus)*, which has a hairy, sterile stamen and light to dark purple flowers.

H. WAYNE PHILLIPS

Hook Violet

HOOK VIOLET
Viola adunca
Violet family (Violaceae)

Description: Like other violets, these flowers look like small pansies, with 2 petals above and 3 below. The united lower petals form a spur, hence the common name. Blossoms are blue or violet, with the side petals having hairs on the inside. The flowers are ¼–¾" long and are attached singly on a slender stalk. Leaves are ¾–1½" long, roundish, and often hairy. The leafy stems may be up to 9¾" tall.

Late spring to midsummer.

Habitat/Range: Common in moist areas such as aspen groves, streamsides, and edges of fields. Found in the montane, subalpine, and alpine ecosystems from Canada to New Mexico.

Comments: Also called Mountain Blue Violet or Purple Violet.

Green Flowers

*This section includes broad-leaved plants
with inconspicuous flowers, as well as large
flowers that are green or have a greenish
cast. Since green flowers grade into white
flowers, readers looking for green flowers
should check the white section as well.*

ROCKY MOUNTAIN NATIONAL PARK

Alpine Nailwort

ALPINE NAILWORT
Paronychia pulvinata
Pink family (Caryophyllaceae)

Description: Light yellowish green, stalkless flowers are embedded in a tight mat of low vegetation. The inconspicuous blossoms lack petals but have 5 sepals, 5 stamens topped with yellow pollen, and papery bracts. Thick basal leaves are longer than wide and are less than ¼" long. The base of the stem is woody. This ground-hugging perennial is less than 2" tall.

Late spring to early summer.

Habitat/Range: Ridges or gravelly and rocky areas of the alpine tundra from Wyoming to New Mexico.

Comments: Formerly known by the scientific name *P. sessiliflora*, this plant was used to cure infections around the fingernails and toenails, hence its common name, Nailwort. The specific name *pulvinata* means "cushionlike." Some botanists place nailwort in the Chickweed family (Alsinaceae).

ROCKY MOUNTAIN NATIONAL PARK

Monument Plant

MONUMENT PLANT
Frasera speciosa
Gentian family (Gentianaceae)

Description: Star-shaped, light green flowers cover the upper portion of a tall, stout stalk. The blossoms usually have 4 sepals, 4 stamens, and 4 pointed petals with dark spots and 2 glands at the base. The ½–1½" wide flowers are on short stalks where the leaves meet the stem. First-year plants lack a flowering stalk, having only a cluster of light green basal leaves that are 10–18" long. On second-year plants, the stem leaves get smaller toward the top of the stem. These whorled leaves are oblong or lance-shaped. This unbranched perennial grows 1–6' tall.

Early to late summer.

Habitat/Range: Found in meadows, pine forests, and on hillsides in the foothills, montane, and subalpine ecosystems from Montana to Mexico.

Comments: Also called Green Gentian, Elkweed (elk eat the leaves), or Deer's Ears (for the shape of the basal leaves).

Heartleaf Twayblade

ROCKY MOUNTAIN NATIONAL PARK

HEARTLEAF TWAYBLADE
Listera cordata ssp. *nephrophylla*
Orchid family (Orchidaceae)

Description: Small, spurless, greenish, whitish, or purplish flowers are arranged in a loose raceme. The long lower lip is cut into 2 narrow, pointed segments. Each segment typically bears a tooth near the base at the outside edge. This plant has only 2 opposite, ½–1¼" long leaves that are heart-shaped. The leaves are stalkless and located at the middle of the 3–10" stem.

Early to late summer.

Habitat/Range: Found in moist forests and along streams in the montane and subalpine ecosystems from Alaska to New Mexico.

Comments: Also called Double-Leaf *(Ophrys nephrophylla).* The common name comes from the English word "tway," which means "two," and "blade," meaning "leaf." The generic name honors Martin Lister, a seventeenth- and eighteenth-century English physician and naturalist.

NORTHERN GREEN BOG ORCHID
Limnorchis hyperborea
Orchid family (Orchidaceae)

Description: A stout stem supports a dense spike of greenish flowers and bracts. The petals and sepals look much alike. The 3 sepals form a hood at the top of the blossom. Two petals stick out to the sides, and the bottom petal forms a lip less than ¼" long, with the narrow spur about the same length. The petals may be tinged with reddish purple. The lance-shaped leaves have parallel veins and are 2–6" long. This plant usually grows 1–2' tall.

Mid- to late summer.

Habitat/Range: Seen along streams and in wet meadows and forests of the foothills, montane, and subalpine ecosystems from Alaska to Colorado.

Comments: The closely related Green Bog Orchid *(L. stricta)* has a shorter, pouch-shaped spur. The specific name *hyperborea* means "of the far north."

Northern Green Bog Orchid

ROCKY MOUNTAIN NATIONAL PARK

LEANNE BENTON

Curly Dock

CURLY DOCK
Rumex crispus
Buckwheat family (Polygonaceae)

Description: A stout stem supports clusters of small, greenish flowers. Each blossom has 6 lobed sepals but no petals. The leaves have wavy edges and may have small teeth. The lance-shaped basal leaves are 6–12" long. The stem leaves are smaller and alternate. This plant grows 1–4' tall.

Early to midsummer.

Habitat/Range: Moist fields and disturbed sites in the foothills and montane ecosystems from Montana to New Mexico.

Comments: Also called Yellowdock, referring to the color of the root. This plant originally came from Europe. The young leaves can be cooked and eaten, while the brown, 3-winged fruits can be crushed and made into flour.

Greenflower Pyrola

GREENFLOWER PYROLA
Pyrola chlorantha
Wintergreen family (Pyrolaceae)

Description: The 3–10 nodding, greenish white flowers typically hang from a slender stem. The blossoms are ⅜–⅝" wide and have 5 petals, 10 stamens, and a curved style that sticks out. The evergreen leaves are ⅜–1½" long and are on stalks about the same length or shorter. The basal leaves are roundish with small round teeth. This perennial grows 4–12" tall.
Mid- to late summer.

Habitat/Range: Moist forests of the montane and subalpine ecosystems from Canada to Arizona.

Comments: Also called Shinleaf *(P. virens)* because the leaves were used as a poultice to lessen the pain of bruised shins. Formerly in the Heath family (Ericaceae).

ONESIDED WINTERGREEN
Orthilia secunda
Wintergreen family (Pyrolaceae)

Description: The 6–20 white or greenish white flowers hang on one side of an often arched stem. The bell-shaped blossoms have 5 petals, 10 stamens, and a straight style that protrudes. The flowers are ¼" long and ¼" across. Shiny basal leaves are ⅜–2½" long on short stalks. The ovate, evergreen leaves have slightly toothed edges. This perennial often grows in groups and reaches 2–10" tall.
Midsummer to early fall.

Habitat/Range: Found in coniferous forests and near streams in the foothills, montane, and subalpine ecosystems from Alaska to New Mexico.

Comments: Also called Sidebells *(Pyrola secunda* or *Ramischia secunda).* Formerly in the Heath family (Ericaceae).

Onesided Wintergreen

ROCKY MOUNTAIN NATIONAL PARK

BRACTED ALUMROOT
Heuchera bracteata
Saxifrage family (Saxifragaceae)

Description: Tiny, greenish blossoms are clustered on one side of a leafless stem. The flowers have 5 sepals and 5 stamens that are longer than the petals. The mainly basal leaves are ¾–1½" wide on long, sticky stalks. The ovate or kidney-shaped leaves usually have 5–7 lobes with sharply pointed teeth. The undersides of the leaves are covered with short, sticky hairs. This perennial grows 4–16" tall.

Late spring to late summer.

Habitat/Range: On and among rocks in the foothills, montane, and subalpine ecosystems of Wyoming and Colorado.

Comments: The generic name honors Johann Heucher, an eighteenth-century German professor of medicine.

Bracted Alumroot

Giant Lousewort

GIANT LOUSEWORT
Pedicularis procera
Snapdragon family (Scrophulariaceae)

Description: Greenish or light yellow flowers with red or purple streaks are interspersed with pointy green bracts. The blossoms are 1–1½" long. The curved upper petal almost touches the wide lower lip. Both basal and stem leaves are pinnately divided into toothed lobes. The fernlike leaves are 8–23" long. The stout stem of this perennial grows 2–4' tall.

Mid- to late summer.

Habitat/Range: Common in forests and meadows of the montane and subalpine ecosystems from Wyoming to New Mexico.

Comments: Also called Gray's Fernleaf Lousewort. The specific name *procera* means "very tall."

RED AND ORANGE FLOWERS

*This section includes red and orange
flowers, as well as those with a maroon or
brownish cast. Since red flowers grade into
pink and purple flowers, readers looking
for red flowers should check the pink and
blue and purple sections as well.*

Burnt-Orange False Dandelion

BURNT-ORANGE FALSE DANDELION
Agoseris aurantiaca
Aster family (Asteraceae)

Description: These 1" wide flowers look like a dandelion that has been dipped in orange paint. The flower color also can be a brownish red. As the blossoms dry, they turn pink or purple. Each leafless stalk bears one flower head that has only ray flowers. The bracts below the flowers are arranged like shingles. The basal leaves are 2–14" long and may be entire or toothed. The narrow leaves and stem both have a milky sap. The stems may be 4–24" tall.

Midsummer.

Habitat/Range: Adds color to meadows and openings in coniferous woods. Found in the foothills, montane, subalpine, and alpine ecosystems from Canada to New Mexico.

Comments: The generic name *Agoseris* means "like a potherb" (a leafy cooked vegetable).

STRAWBERRY BLITE
Chenopodium capitatum
Goosefoot family (Chenopodiaceae)

Description: Tiny flowers in rounded clusters decorate the smooth stem of this annual. The blossoms lack petals, but have sepals that turn blood red as the flowers mature. Smooth green leaves are shaped like arrowheads. The alternate leaves bear coarse teeth. Stems may be branched or simple and grow 4–24" in height.

Midsummer.

Habitat/Range: This nonnative plant is found in moist, disturbed ground along roads, in burned areas, and near abandoned buildings. It grows in the foothills, montane, and subalpine ecosystems from Alaska to New Mexico.

Comments: Also called Indian Paint. The family name comes from the shape of the plant's leaves. This plant is related to spinach and beets; the leaves and fruits are edible.

Strawberry Blite

KING'S CROWN
Rhodiola integrifolia
Stonecrop family (Crassulaceae)

Description: A flat-topped cluster of deep red to maroon flowers sits atop a succulent, leafy stalk. The 4–5 pointed petals are ⅛–½" long. Numerous smooth, fleshy leaves are ⅜–1" long. The alternate leaves are flat with an oblong shape. Leaves are ungrooved. Clustered, unbranched stems are 2–12" tall.

Midsummer.

Habitat/Range: Found in moist or gravelly meadows in the subalpine and alpine ecosystems from Alaska to New Mexico.

Comments: Also called Roseroot because its root has a roselike scent. The former name was *Sedum rosea*. The plant looks similar to Rose Crown *(Clementsia rhodantha)*, which has pink flowers.

King's Crown

Mountain Wood Lily

MOUNTAIN WOOD LILY
Lilium philadelphicum
Lily family (Liliaceae)

Description: These large, showy blossoms have 6 orange-red tepals. The tepals are 2–2⅜" long and bear dark spots at their bases. Usually, 1–3 flowers top each stem. The smooth leaves have parallel veins. The top leaves are arranged in a whorl and the rest of the leaves are alternate. Stems arise from bulbs and may be 11–24" tall. Fruits are cylindrical capsules.

Midsummer.

Habitat/Range: On hillsides and in open woods in the foothills to upper montane ecosystems from Canada to New Mexico.

Comments: Also called Tiger Lily. The colorful blossoms often attract butterflies and hummingbirds.

Pinedrops

PINEDROPS
Pterospora andromedea
Pinesap family (Monotropaceae)

Description: This plant lacks chlorophyll, the photosynthetic pigment that gives plants their green color. A raceme of bell-shaped flowers dangles from a conspicuous, reddish brown stem. The blossoms have 5 cream-colored lobes, 5 red sepals, and 10 stamens. The scalelike leaves are ¼–1" long. Stout, unbranched stem is covered with sticky hairs. The plants grow 7–31" tall. Clusters of dried stems persist into the winter.

Early to late summer.

Habitat/Range: Grows on the forest floor, particularly under conifers. Can be found in the foothills and montane ecosystems from Canada to Mexico.

Comments: Formerly included in the Heath family (Ericaceae), this parasitic plant lives in association with fungi that break down dead vegetation.

BROWNIE LADYSLIPPER
Cypripedium fasciculatum
Orchid family (Orchidaceae)

Description: The bottom petal of this unusual flower forms a yellowish green sac with purple markings. The other 2 petals and brownish purple sepals look alike. The bottom 2 sepals are united. Usually, 2–4 drooping flowers 1–1½" long are found on each stem. There are 2 opposite, roundish leaves that are 2–6" long. The plants often grow in clusters 2–8" tall.

Spring to midsummer.

Habitat/Range: Relatively rare, the plant is seen in coniferous forests and on hillsides in the montane and subalpine ecosystems from Canada to Colorado.

Comments: Also called Clustered Ladyslipper. Many ladyslippers are rare as they have very specific habitat requirements. The name *Cypripedium* means "Venus slipper." Some botanists place this species in the Ladyslipper family (Cypripediaceae).

LORAINE YEATTS

Brownie Ladyslipper

SPOTTED CORALROOT
Corallorhiza maculata
Orchid family (Orchidaceae)

Description: This reddish brown plant lacks chlorophyll. Up to 30 flowers are arranged in a raceme. The flowers grow to ¾" long with 3 brownish purple sepals and 2 similarly colored petals. The base of the spotted, white lip has 2 teeth. Its reduced leaves are scalelike. An unbranched, reddish brown or yellowish, fleshy stem grows 6–24" in height. The plants often are found in clumps.

Late spring to late summer.

Habitat/Range: Fairly common in shady, moist forests in the foothills, montane, and subalpine ecosystems from Canada to Guatemala.

Comments: Striped Coralroot *(C. striata)* looks similar, but its flower is striped instead of spotted. People have used the rhizome—the elongate subterranean stem—as a tea to reduce fevers and act as a sedative.

Spotted Coralroot

Alpine Sorrel

ALPINE SORREL
Oxyria digyna
Buckwheat family (Polygonaceae)

Description: Numerous tiny flowers are tightly clustered at the top of the stem. The ¹⁄₁₆" long flowers lack petals, but have green or red sepals with 4 lobes. The mainly basal leaves are kidney-shaped and entire. The fleshy, long-stalked leaves are smooth and up to 1" in diameter. The small, reddish fruits are round and winged. A simple stem usually is 4–12" tall.

Mid- to late summer.

Habitat/Range: Found in moist, shady areas, including areas beneath boulders and between rocks, in the montane, subalpine, and alpine ecosystems from Alaska to Arizona.

Comments: The name *Oxyria* is derived from a Greek word meaning "sour." It refers to the taste of the leaves, which are high in oxalate and vitamin C.

Western Scarlet Gilia

WESTERN SCARLET GILIA
Ipomosis aggregata ssp. *aggregata*
Phlox family (Polemoniaceae)

Description: Long clusters of red, trumpet-shaped flowers top slender stems. The flowers are ¾–2" long and have 5 pointed lobes. Alternate leaves are 1–2½" long and sticky. When crushed, the pinnately divided leaves have a skunky smell. The upper stem leaves are smaller and narrow. This biennial often grows in groups and reaches 1–3' tall.

Late spring to early fall.

Habitat/Range: Common in dry fields and open forests, on gravelly slopes, and along roads in the foothills and montane ecosystems from Montana to New Mexico.

Comments: Also called Fairy Trumpets or Skyrocket Gilia, formerly *Gilia aggregata*. Scarlet Gilia hybridizes with the closely related *I. aggregata* ssp. *candida*, which has cream-colored blossoms, to produce a plant with pink flowers.

WESTERN RED COLUMBINE
Aquilegia elegantula
Buttercup family (Ranunculaceae)

Description: These beautiful flowers have 5 red, petal-like sepals and 5 yellow, funnel-shaped petals with red spurs. The drooping blossoms are 1" long with many yellow stamens that protrude from the flower. Leaves are mainly basal and smooth. The compound leaves are divided into 3 segments, each segment being 3-lobed. Slender stems are 4–16" tall.

Late spring to late summer.

Habitat/Range: Found in moist areas, open woods, and hillsides in the upper foothills, montane, and subalpine ecosystems of Utah, New Mexico, and Colorado.

Comments: Some botanists place columbines in the Hellebore family (Helleboraceae). This plant looks much like the larger Red or Crimson Columbine *(A. formosa)*, found from Alaska to Utah.

Western Red Columbine

ROCKY MOUNTAIN NATIONAL PARK

Narrowleaf Paintbrush

NARROWLEAF PAINTBRUSH
Castilleja linariaefolia
Snapdragon family (Scrophulariaceae)

Description: As with other paintbrushes, the colorful part of the plant consists of bracts and sepals. The hairy red sepals of this species have a deep slit on the lower side. A cluster of bright red, deeply lobed bracts and yellowish green flowers grows atop a branched stem. The red-tinged, green corolla is 2-lipped and more than 1" long. Alternate leaves are very narrow and entire or with lobes. The leaves have one main vein and are 1½–4" long. This perennial grows 1–3' tall.

Early to late summer.

Habitat/Range: Common, found growing on rocky hillsides, among shrubs, and in meadows and open forests in the foothills and montane ecosystems from Wyoming to New Mexico.

Comments: Also called Wyoming Paintbrush. Many kinds of paintbrush are partially parisitic on the roots of other plants such as Sage *(Artemesia).*

Scarlet Paintbrush

SCARLET PAINTBRUSH
Castilleja miniata
Snapdragon family (Scrophulariaceae)

Description: Like other paintbrushes, the colorful part of the plant is composed of bracts and sepals. A dense cluster of crimson bracts and green flowers grows atop a branched stem. The green corolla is 2-lipped, inconspicuous, and less than 1¼" long. The colored bracts typically have 3 deep lobes. Alternate leaves have 3 main veins and are 1–2⅜" long. The leaves are entire, or the upper leaves may be lobed. Grows 1–3' tall.

Late spring to late summer.

Habitat/Range: Common in moist meadows, open woods, and among shrubs in the foothills, montane, and subalpine ecosystems from Canada to New Mexico.

Comments: Also called Giant Red Paintbrush. Foothills Paintbrush *(C. integra)* is a common orange-bracted variety.

WHIPPLE PENSTEMON
Penstemon whippleanus
Snapdragon family (Scrophulariaceae)

Description: Nodding clusters of dark reddish purple or sometimes whitish, 2-lipped flowers grow atop a leafy stem. The outside surfaces of the ¾–1½" long blossoms are covered with sticky hairs. The 3-lobed bottom lip is longer than the 2-lobed upper lip. A tuft of hairs decorates the tip of the 5th, sterile, stamen. Smooth, opposite leaves are ½–6" long. The stalked lower leaves are oval shaped while the upper leaves have no stalk. The dark green leaves usually are entire, but sometimes have teeth. Plants grow from 4–28" in height.

Midsummer to early fall.

Habitat/Range: Grows on gravelly slopes and in meadows and open woods in the montane, subalpine, and alpine ecosystems from Montana to New Mexico.

Comments: Also called Dusky or Dark Beardtongue.

Whipple Penstemon

PINK FLOWERS

ROCKY MOUNTAIN NATIONAL PARK

This section includes flowers grading from pale pinkish white to vivid electric pink and rose purple. Since pink flowers grade into white and purple flowers, readers looking for pink flowers should check the blue and purple and white sections as well.

Geyer Onion

GEYER ONION
Allium geyeri
Onion family (Alliaceae)

Description: Like other onions, this plant has flower parts in multiples of 3 and leaves with parallel veins. The species has an erect cluster of pink or sometimes white flowers. The stamens do not stick out past the small petals and sepals. Usually, 2–3 papery bracts lie below the flowers. There are 3 or more grasslike basal leaves with each leafless flower stalk. Plants may grow 4–23" tall. The edible bulbs and foliage have the typical scent of onions.

Early to late summer.

Habitat/Range: Meadows and hillsides in the foothills, montane, subalpine, and alpine ecosystems from Canada to New Mexico.

Comments: In North America, scientists discovered evidence of indigenous people using wild onions as food 6,000 years ago. Native Americans ate the young leaves and bulbs raw or cooked. The distinctive onion smell helps harvesters distinguish onions from the poisonous Death Camas.

Nodding Onion

NODDING ONION
Allium cernuum
Onion family (Alliaceae)

Description: Like other members of the Lily group, onions have flower parts in multiples of 3 and leaves with parallel veins. A nodding cluster of flowers is a distinctive characteristic of this species. The leafless flower stalk may be 6–23" tall. The stamens stick out past the small pink or white tepals. Usually, 2 papery bracts cover the buds and fall off by the time the flowers bloom. Grasslike basal leaves are 2–10" long. The edible bulbs, like the rest of the foliage, have the typical scent of onions.

Early summer to early fall.

Habitat/Range: Grassy fields and slopes in the foothills, montane, and subalpine ecosystems from Canada to Mexico.

Comments: Explorers from both Stephen Long's and Prince Maximilian's nineteenth-century expeditions ate wild onion leaves to cure an illness that probably was scurvy.

Showy Milkweed

SHOWY MILKWEED
Asclepius speciosa
Milkweed family (Asclepiadaceae)

Description: This plant's baseball-sized clusters of pink or whitish flowers are hard to miss. The ¾" wide blossoms have 5 sepals, 5 bent-down petals, and 5 curved, horned hoods that look like petals. Simple, 3–8" long leaves are lance-shaped, ovate, or oblong. The thick, opposite leaves have short stalks and obvious veins. After fertilization, pods grow to 2–4½" long. These are covered with short, white hairs and split open to release plumed brown seeds. Stems with milky sap grow 1–5' tall.
Early to midsummer.

Habitat/Range: Found in fields, along roads, and in ditches in the foothills and montane ecosystems from Canada to Arizona.

Comments: Also called Pink or Common Milkweed. The striped black, yellow, and white caterpillars of monarch butterflies feed on milkweed foliage.

BEAUTIFUL DAISY
Erigeron elatior
Aster family (Asteraceae)

Description: Numerous narrow ray flowers are lavender or pink and surround a yellow center. There are 1–3 heads per stem. Bracts around the flower heads are about equal in length, with pink, woolly hairs. The simple, entire leaves are lance-shaped and more than ¾" wide. Upper leaves clasp the stem. The leafy stems are sticky-hairy toward the top. This perennial plant may be up to 24" tall.
Mid- to late summer.

Habitat/Range: Along streams and other moist areas in the montane and subalpine forests of Colorado and Utah.

Comments: Also called Pink Daisy or Tall Fleabane. The similar Coulter Daisy *(E. coulteri)* has bracts with thick dark hairs, white ray flowers, and hairy, serrate leaves.

Beautiful Daisy

ROCKY MOUNTAIN NATIONAL PARK

Kansas Gayfeather

KANSAS GAYFEATHER
Liatris punctata
Aster family (Asteraceae)

Description: Showy, pink to lavender clusters of gayfeathers brighten meadows in late summer. As many as 100 5-lobed flowers are crowded along the top of the stem in heads ¾" long. Each flower head contains 3–8 disk flowers surrounded by overlapping bracts. Leaves are very narrow, 1–5" long, and have tiny dots on the underside. The clustered, unbranched stems may be 6–32" tall. Seeds have feathery bristles.

Late summer to early fall.

Habitat/Range: Dry meadows in the foothills and montane ecosystems from Canada to Mexico. Seen from Michigan to Arkansas in the eastern United States.

Comments: Also called Blazing Star, Dotted Gayfeather, or Button Snakeroot. The word "feather" in this plant's name refers to each flower's two featherlike style branches.

Rosy Pussytoes

ROSY PUSSYTOES
Antennaria rosea
Aster family (Asteraceae)

Description: Flower heads that look and feel like the pads of a cat's paw give this plant its common name. Heads contain only disk flowers and are less than ¼" tall. The bracts around the flower heads usually are pink tipped or sometimes white tipped. Primarily basal leaves are up to ¾" long with woolly hairs. The leaves are rounded at the tip and narrow toward the base. The light gray-green vegetation spreads by runners to form mats. Stems are 8–16" tall.

Late spring to late summer.

Habitat/Range: Meadows and open woods in the foothills, montane, subalpine, and alpine ecosystems from Alaska to New Mexico.

Comments: *Antennaria* means "like antennae." One plant usually has all male flowers or all female flowers.

ROCKY MOUNTAIN BEEPLANT
Cleome serrulata
Caper family (Capparaceae)

Description: A cluster of 4-petalled, pink to lavender—or occasionally white—flowers blooms atop a branched stem. The flowers are ¼-½" long with protruding stamens. The leaves are alternate and compound with lance-shaped leaflets that are ³⁄₁₆" to just over ⅜" wide. The lower leaves have long stalks. The ½-3⅛" seedpods dangle below the flowers. This annual usually grows 1-3' tall.

Mid- to late summer.

Habitat/Range: Common in sandy meadows, near roads, and along trails in the foothills and montane ecosystems from Canada to New Mexico.

Comments: Also called Pink Cleome or Stinkweed due to the unpleasant smell of the foliage. It is related to the garden plant Spiderflower. This plant is in the same family as Capers *(Capparis spinosa)*, which are used as seasoning in the dish chicken piccata.

Rocky Mountain Beeplant

Mountain Ball Cactus

MOUNTAIN BALL CACTUS
Pediocactus simpsonii var. *minor*
Cactus family (Cactaceae)

Description: Beautiful rose-colored flowers top this small, ball-shaped cactus. The fragrant flowers have many pointed petals and numerous stamens. Cactus spines actually are modified leaves. Fleshy stems are 2–6" in diameter with nipple-like projections called tubercles. The tubercles lack grooves on the upper side.

Mid- to late spring.

Habitat/Range: Dry, sandy soil of meadows and sunny pine forests in the foothills and montane ecosystems from Montana to New Mexico.

Comments: Formerly *Echinocactus simpsonii*. The similar Ball Cactus *(Coryphantha vivipara)* has a groove on the top of the tubercles and is found on the plains. Hen-and-Chickens Cactus *(Echinocereus viridiflorus)* has greenish yellow flowers.

Twinflower

TWINFLOWER
Linnaea borealis
Honeysuckle family (Caprifoliaceae)

Description: These dainty, ¼–⅝" long, pink or white, bell-shaped flowers have 5 lobes. The fragrant, paired blossoms dangle from a 2–4", forked, leafless stalk. The opposite, evergreen leaves are roundish, entire or slightly toothed, and less than 1" long. Its semiwoody, creeping stems lie flat on the ground, forming mats of vegetation.

Mid- to late summer.

Habitat/Range: Graces moist, shady areas and evergreen forests in the montane and subalpine ecosystems. In North America, this circumboreal plant can be found from Alaska to New Mexico and east to West Virginia.

Comments: The generic name honors Carolus Linnaeus, the Swedish botanist who developed the two-name system for designating plants and animals.

MOSS CAMPION
Silene acaulis ssp. *subacaulescens*
Pink family (Caryophyllaceae)

Description: Numerous tiny flowers form a mass of pink blossoms on a pincushion-like cluster of leaves. The 5 petals have a small notch at the tip. The ¼" wide, tubular flowers have such a short stalk that the blossoms barely rise above the tiny leaves. The opposite, pointed leaves are mosslike and ¼–¾" long. The mat of vegetation may reach 1' across and 1–2⅜" tall.

Early to late summer.

Habitat/Range: A pioneer species in windy, rocky fellfields on the alpine tundra from Canada to New Mexico. Also found in similar areas around the globe.

Comments: Also called Cushion Pink or Dwarf Catchfly. Flowers are sometimes white. An individual plant might not flower until it is 10 years old; a large cushion covered with blossoms may be 25 years old.

Moss Campion

ROSE CROWN
Clementsia rhodantha
Stonecrop family (Crassulaceae)

Description: A tight cluster of pink or almost white flowers sits atop a succulent, leafy stalk. The 4–5 pointed petals are ⅜–½" long. Numerous smooth, fleshy leaves are ½–1" long. The alternate leaves are flat with an oblong shape. Leaves are grooved on top. Clustered, unbranched stems are 6–12" tall.

Midsummer.

Habitat/Range: Adds beauty to wet meadows in the subalpine and alpine ecosystems from Montana to New Mexico.

Comments: Also called Queen's Crown. The former generic name was *Sedum*. Looks similar to King's Crown *(Rodiola integrifolia)*, which has red flowers. The foliage of both plants turns red in the fall.

Rose Crown

ROCKY MOUNTAIN NATIONAL PARK

Swamp Laurel

SWAMP LAUREL
Kalmia microphylla
Heath family (Ericaceae)

Description: Clusters of deep pink, cup-shaped flowers are ⅜–¾" across. The blossoms have 5 lobes and 10 stamens. The opposite, evergreen leaves are dark green above with light-colored hairs below. The simple, ½–1½" long leaves are entire, with the edges often rolled under. Woody, branched stems are 4–18" tall and form mats over the ground.

Mid- to late summer.

Habitat/Range: Uncommon, but may be profuse at the edges of streams and ponds and in wet areas in the subalpine and alpine ecosystems. Found from Canada to Colorado.

Comments: Also called Pale, Bog, or Alpine Laurel. The pollen-bearing anthers are protected in small pouches until maturity. The weight of an insect or expansion of the flower releases the anthers.

ALPINE CLOVER
Trifolium dasyphyllum
Bean family (Fabaceae)

Description: The top petal of these ⅜–¾" long flowers is white or cream colored. The other petals are pink or purple. Typically, 10–30 pealike blossoms are borne in a rounded cluster atop a leafless stem. Under the flower head are green-and-white bracts. The basal leaves have 3 very narrow, folded leaflets that are less than 1" long. The leaflets are entire and very hairy, particularly on the underside. This mat plant is 1–6" tall and grows in clumps.

Mid- to late summer.

Habitat/Range: Common in windy, rocky areas of the subalpine and alpine ecosystems from Montana to New Mexico.

Comments: Also called Whiproot Clover. *Trifolium* means "three leaves" (leaflets) and *dasyphyllum* means "shaggy or hairy plant."

Alpine Clover

H. WAYNE PHILLIPS

Kinnikinnick

KINNIKINNICK
Arctostaphylos uva-ursi ssp. *adenotricha*
Heath family (Ericaceae)

Description: Tiny, urn-shaped flowers dangle in groups from short branches. Waxy, white and/ or pink blossoms are less than ¼" long and have 5 lobes. Leathery, evergreen leaves are ¼–1" long and alternate. The leaves are entire, ovate, and widest toward the tip. Stems are woody and creeping with peeling, reddish bark. Stem branches have long, sticky hairs. The plant may be up to 6" tall. The fruit is a pea-sized red berry.

Spring to early summer.

Habitat/Range: Forms a ground cover under evergreen forests in the foothills, montane, and subalpine ecosystems from Alaska to New Mexico.

Comments: Also called Bearberry or Manzanita. Native Americans smoked the dried leaves of Kinnikinnick mixed with the bark of Red Osier Dogwood *(Swida sericea)*. When cooked slowly, the bland berries pop like popcorn. Deer and bighorn sheep browse on the evergreen leaves and twigs in winter. Songbirds, turkeys, grouse, rodents, and bears eat the berries.

LORAINE YEATTS

Colorado Loco

COLORADO LOCO
Oxytropis lambertii
Bean family (Fabaceae)

Description: Like all loco flowers, these blossoms are pea-like, with the tip of the keel pointed. Brilliant, ½–1" long magenta flowers are clustered in tight groups atop a leafless stalk. The sepals and beanlike fruit have white hairs. Leaves are pinnately compound with 7–17 leaflets covered with silvery hairs. The plants are 4–16" in height.

Early to late summer.

Habitat/Range: Common in fields in the foothills, montane, and subalpine ecosystems from Canada to Texas. In places, it turns meadows into seas of magenta.

Comments: Also called Lambert's Crazyweed or Purple Locoweed. May hybridize with Rocky Mountain Loco *(O. sericea)* to produce whitish lavender flowers. May be confused with Parry's Loco *(O. parryi)*, which is a shorter, more sparsely flowered alpine variety.

PARRY CLOVER
Trifolium parryi
Bean family (Fabaceae)

Description: Fragrant rose-purple or reddish purple flowers are ½–¾" long. Usually, 6–20 pealike flowers are clustered in each large, round head. Below the heads are whitish, papery bracts. The leaves are primarily basal with 3 leaflets. The smooth leaflets may be entire or toothed. Grows to 6" tall and forms clumps of vegetation.

Mid- to late summer.

Habitat/Range: Common in moist meadows of the subalpine and alpine ecosystems from Montana to Colorado.

Comments: Also called Rose Clover. This and a number of other plants are named in honor of Charles Parry. The nineteenth-century botanist spent forty summers collecting plants in the western United States. The low-growing Dwarf Clover *(T. nanum)* has only 1–4 flowers per head.

LORAINE YEATTS

Parry Clover

LORAINE YEATTS

Fewflower Loco

FEWFLOWER LOCO
Oxytropis multiceps
Bean family (Fabaceae)

Description: As its common name implies, there are only 1–4 flowers on each short stalk. Like all loco flowers, these blossoms are pea-like, with the tip of the keel pointed. The ½–1" long flowers are rose pink or purple with pink sepals that inflate to enclose the ripe fruit. Pinnately compound leaves have 5–9 leaflets covered with gray hairs. The ¾–4" plant grows in clumps.

Late spring to late summer.

Habitat/Range: Dry, gravelly slopes in the foothills, montane, and subalpine ecosystems from Wyoming to Colorado.

Comments: Also called Tufted Loco. Horses and cattle only eat locoweed if better forage is unavailable. After eating quantities of the plant, the animals act crazily, hence the name.

DENVER BOTANIC GARDENS

Whorled Loco

WHORLED LOCO
Oxytropis splendens
Bean family (Fabaceae)

Description: Numerous rose-pink, dark blue, or purple flowers are bunched in woolly clusters atop a hairy stem. The ¼–⅝" long blossoms occasionally are white with purple on the tip of the keel. Like all loco flowers, these blossoms are pea-like, with the tip of the keel pointed. Both sepals and pods have white hairs. Some of the leaflets are arranged in circles around the stem. The plants grow 4–14" tall.

Early to midsummer.

Habitat/Range: Common in dry, rocky meadows and aspen groves in the montane and subalpine ecosystems from Canada to New Mexico.

Comments: Also called Showy Loco.

ROSE GENTIAN
Gentianella acuta
Gentian family (Gentianaceae)

Description: These ¼–¾" long, tubular flowers come in a range of colors: yellowish white, rose, blue, or lavender. The blossoms have 4–5 pointed lobes with a fringe of hairs inside the flower. Each flower is borne on a slender stalk. Opposite leaves are attached directly to the slender stem. The smooth leaves are ¼–1½" long. The erect, leafy stem may be simple or branched. Plants are 2–16" tall.

Early to late summer.

Habitat/Range: Stream banks and moist meadows in the foothills, montane, subalpine, and alpine ecosystems from Alaska to Mexico.

Comments: Also called Little or Northern Gentian *(G. amarella)*. Engelmann Gentian *(G. heterosepala)* has sepal lobes of two different sizes. The short, alpine Oneflower Gentian *(Comastoma tenellum)* has small blue flowers. The white, yellow, or blue flowers of Marsh Gentian *(G. strictiflora)* have a very short stalk or none at all.

Rose Gentian

FREMONT GERANIUM
Geranium caespitosum
Geranium family (Geraniaceae)

Description: The 5 pink to lavender petals have purple veins that guide bees to nectar and pollen. The flowers are 1½" wide with long, soft hairs on part of their length. Blossoms have 5 sepals and 10 stamens. Palmately lobed leaves are divided into 5–7 toothed segments. Sticky hairs cover the 4–30" stems, which grow in clusters. The seeds may be up to 1⅛" long.

Late spring to late summer.

Habitat/Range: Common along forest edges, in dry meadows, and on slopes in the foothills, montane, and subalpine ecosystems from Wyoming to Mexico.

Comments: *Geranium* comes from a Greek word meaning "crane." This refers to the long seeds, which look like a crane's bill. Also called Common Wild Geranium. The "Fremont" in the common name refers to John Charles Fremont, who collected this and many other plants during his nineteenth-century western expeditions.

Fremont Geranium

WAX CURRANT
Ribes cereum
Gooseberry family (Grossulariaceae)

Description: Fragrant pink, tubular flowers about ¼" long grace this shrub. The hairy blossoms have 5 lobes. Leaves have 3–5 shallow, toothed lobes. The alternate leaves typically are less than 1½" wide. This plant has sticky hairs but lacks thorns. Grows 20–78" tall. Fleshy, reddish orange berries ripen in midsummer.

Late spring to midsummer.

Habitat/Range: Common on dry hillsides and in pine forests of the foothills and montane ecosystems from Canada to New Mexico.

Comments: The Zunis, Hopis, and other Native Americans collected the berries of this and other currants. They ate the berries cooked, dried, or raw. Today, people mix the currants with sugar to make jam. Bears, rodents, and many species of birds eat currants. Deer and elk browse the green leaves.

ROCKY MOUNTAIN NATIONAL PARK

Wax Currant

Horsemint

HORSEMINT
Monarda fistulosa var. *menthifolia*
Mint family (Lamiaceae)

Description: Many pink to purple, 2-lipped flowers are clustered in a rounded head atop a square stem. Stamens stick out beyond the petals. The heads are 1–3" across. Under the 1–1½" long flowers lie leafy bracts. The toothed, ovate leaves are fragrant, hairy, and opposite. The typically unbranched stems grow 1–3' tall.
Midsummer.

Habitat/Range: On sunny slopes, along roadsides, and the edges of aspen forests in the foothills and montane ecosystems from Canada to Texas.

Comments: Also called Wild Bergamot or Beebalm because it is a favorite haunt of bees, butterflies, and hummingbirds. The Lakotas made a tea from the flowers for colds and fevers. The leaves can also be made into a tea or eaten cooked.

WOUNDWORT
Stachys palustris ssp. *pilosa*
Mint family (Lamiaceae)

Description: White, pink, or lavender, 2-lipped flowers appear in several tiers of whorls at the top of a square, hairy stem. There usually are 2–6 flowers in each whorl. Darker spots decorate the bottom lip of the ⅜–⅝" long blossoms. Each flower has 5 sepal lobes and 4 stamens. The toothed, ovate leaves are 1½–3¼" long and hairy. This perennial grows 6–31" tall.
Early to late summer.

Habitat/Range: Moist soil of meadows and streamsides in the foothills and montane ecosystems from Canada to New Mexico.

Comments: Also called Hedge Nettle. The specific name *palustris* means "of marshes." People have used this plant to relieve colic, heal wounds, and as a yellow dye.

Woundwort

COMMON FIREWEED
Chamerion danielsii
Evening Primrose family (Onagraceae)

Description: Showy, bright pink to rose-purple flowers are arranged in racemes atop tall, leafy stems. The 4 petals form a blossom that is 1" across. Its 4-lobed stigma is a common feature of this family's members. The lowest flowers in the raceme bloom first and are the first to form narrow pods 2–3" long. When ripe, the pods open to release tiny, plumed seeds into the wind. Lance-shaped, alternate leaves are 2–6" long with prominent veins. The mainly unbranched stems may grow from 20" to a towering 7' tall.

Early summer to early fall.

Habitat/Range: Locally abundant in burned areas, along roadsides and streamsides, in disturbed soil, and along forest edges in the foothills, montane, and subalpine ecosystems from Alaska to New Mexico.

Comments: Also called Willow-Herb or Blooming Sally *(Epilobium angustifolium).*

Common Fireweed

Fairy Slipper

FAIRY SLIPPER
Calypso bulbosa
Orchid family (Orchidaceae)

Description: These fragrant pink flowers have a slipper-shaped lip, hence its common name. The central petal is whitish pink with yellow and reddish purple markings. The other 2 petals and 3 sepals look similar. A single drooping flower 1¼" long sits atop a reddish stem. The 2–8" stem has a tubelike sheath around it. A single basal leaf often appears after the flower is finished blooming. The oval leaf is 1¼–2½" long.

Spring to midsummer.

Habitat/Range: Rare, but may be abundant in spots. Grows in moist, shady evergreen forests in the foothills, montane, and subalpine ecosystems from Alaska to New Mexico.

Comments: Also called Venus's Slipper or Calypso Orchid. Some botanists place this species in the Ladyslipper family (Cypripediaceae).

Tufted Broomrape

TUFTED BROOMRAPE
Aphyllon fasciculatum
Broomrape family (Orobanchaceae)

Description: This plant usually bears 4–10 stalked, pinkish, dull yellow, or light purple flowers. The 5-lobed blossoms are ½–1¼" long. Alternate leaves are small and scalelike. Thick, pinkish stalks are fleshy and covered with sticky hairs. This perennial lacks chlorophyll and is parasitic on roots of sages *(Artemesia)* and other members of the Aster family (Asteraceae). Grows 1–6" tall.

Late spring to midsummer.

Habitat/Range: Found in dry meadows and on hillsides in the foothills and montane ecosystems from Canada to New Mexico.

Comments: Also called Cancer Root *(Orobanche fasciculata)*. The Paiutes of Utah ate the stems.

MANY-FLOWERED PHLOX
Phlox multiflora
Phlox family (Polemoniaceae)

Description: Low mats of vegetation bear numerous pink, light blue, or white blossoms. Each ½" wide flower has 5 petals united at the base, 5 sepals, and a 3-lobed style. Narrow, opposite leaves are ¼–1¼" long with entire margins. The simple leaves are smooth except for fine hairs at their base. Branched stems are ¾–4" tall and grow in clumps. The base of the stems are woody.

Late spring to midsummer.

Habitat/Range: Common in grassy areas, pine forests, and on slopes in the foothills, montane, subalpine, and alpine ecosystems from Montana to New Mexico.

Comments: Also called Rocky Mountain Phlox. Alpine or Cushion Phlox *(P. sibirica* ssp. *pulvinata)* has broader, shorter leaves with sticky hairs and grows mainly in alpine areas.

Many-Flowered Phlox

PINK SPRING BEAUTY
Claytonia rosea
Purslane family (Portulacaceae)

Description: Three or more pink or white flowers ¼–¾" wide grow atop each slender stem. The blossoms have 2 sepals, a 3-parted style, and 5 petals with dark pink veins. The stems usually have 2 narrow, opposite, lance-shaped leaves ¾–3½" long. There also is at least 1 smooth basal leaf. The delicate plant grows 2–9" tall.

Early spring to midsummer.

Habitat/Range: An early spring bloomer in the moist soil of the foothills. Also found under pines and in meadows up to the alpine ecosystem from Canada to New Mexico.

Comments: Native Americans ate the bulblike corms. Grizzly bears also favor the corms.

Pink Spring Beauty

Alpine Primrose

ALPINE PRIMROSE
Primula angustifolia
Primrose family (Primulaceae)

Description: These brilliant pink, 5-petaled flowers have yellow centers. The occasionally white blossoms have a small notch at the tip of the petals. One fragrant flower usually is attached to a stalk that is under 4" tall. The blossoms are ¾" across. Rosettes of narrow basal leaves grow in clumps. The thick, entire leaves are folded.

Late spring to midsummer.

Habitat/Range: Common in rocky fellfields and meadows in the subalpine and alpine ecosystems of Colorado and New Mexico.

Comments: Also called Fairy Primrose.

Parry Primrose

PARRY PRIMROSE
Primula parryi
Primrose family (Primulaceae)

Description: Its beautiful magenta flowers tower over other alpine plants, making this a favorite of mountain climbers. The 5-petaled flowers are ⅝–1¼" across with yellow centers. The blossoms have a small notch at the tip of the petals. Usually, 3–12 flowers are grouped in a long cluster atop a stout, leafless stalk. The 2–12" long basal leaves are arranged in a rosette and stand upright. The thick, smooth leaves are oblong. Plants grow 3–16" tall.

Midsummer.

Habitat/Range: Wet meadows, near boulders, and along streamsides in the subalpine and alpine ecosystems from Montana to New Mexico.

Comments: Flowers and foliage may have a cloying odor.

SHOOTING STAR
Dodecatheon pulchellum
Primrose family (Primulaceae)

Description: Shooting Star is a fitting name for these unique, bright rose-pink blossoms. Each flower has 4–5 petals, bent sharply backward, revealing a yellow center inscribed with a wiggly, reddish purple line. The 5 stamens form a dartlike point. One or more ¾–1½" long flowers are attached to each leafless stalk. Around the stalk is a cluster of basal leaves that are 1¼–12" long. The smooth, oblong leaves usually are entire but may be barely toothed. Plants grow 4–16" tall.

Spring to midsummer.

Habitat/Range: Abundant along streamsides and in moist meadows in the foothills, montane, subalpine, and alpine ecosystems from Alaska to Mexico.

Comments: Also called American Cyclamen. The Thompson Indian name for this plant means "beautiful maiden." The Okanagan people called it "Curlew's Bill."

Shooting Star

BOG PYROLA
Pyrola rotundifolia ssp. *asarifolia*
Wintergreen family (Pyrolaceae)

Description: Nodding, pink to rose-purple, waxy flowers are arranged in a tall raceme. Each blossom is less than ½" across and has 5 petals, 10 stamens, and a long, curved style. Roundish leaves are basal or located near the base of the stem. The stalked, leathery leaves are green above and brownish below. The leaves may be up to 3½" long with tiny rounded teeth. This plant can grow to 16" tall.

Midsummer.

Habitat/Range: Wet, shady ground of streamsides, bogs, springs, and coniferous forests in the foothills, montane, and subalpine ecosystems from Alaska to New Mexico.

Comments: Also called Alpine Pyrola, Pink Pyrola, or Swamp Wintergreen. Pyrolas used to be in the Heath family (Ericaceae).

ROCKY MOUNTAIN NATIONAL PARK

Bog Pyrola

Pink Plumes

PINK PLUMES
Erythrocoma triflora
Rose family (Rosaceae)

Description: From 3–6 bell-shaped, rose-pink flowers dangle from a reddish, hairy stalk. The obvious parts of the ½" long blossoms are the bracts and sepals. Pale pink, yellow, or white petals barely stick out. The pinnately compound leaves are 4–8" long and primarily basal. The 9–19 hairy leaflets are cut into 3–5 toothed segments. After being pollinated, the blossoms turn upwards and a tuft of feathery-tailed seeds develops. Stems may grow 6–24" tall.

Midspring to midsummer.

Habitat/Range: Found in meadows, aspen forests, and on hillsides in the foothills, montane, and subalpine ecosystems from Canada to New Mexico.

Comments: Also called Prairie Smoke, Old-Man's Whiskers, Torch Flower, or Three-Flowered Avens, formerly *Geum ciliatum* or *G. triflorum.*

Wild Rose

WILD ROSE
Rosa woodsii
Rose family (Rosaceae)

Description: Fragrant, 5-petaled pink blossoms with many yellow stamens adorn this thorny shrub. The 1½–2½" wide flowers usually appear in clusters of 2 or more. The 5 sticky sepals dry out and stay attached to the edible red fruit, which is called a "hip." Alternate, pinnately compound leaves have 5 or more toothed leaflets and stipules at the base of the leaf stalk. The woody, branched stems bear thorns that are wide at the base. The round, hard hips stay on the shrub into the wintertime. This plant usually grows 3–5' tall, but may grow taller.

Late spring to late summer.

Habitat/Range: Found in meadows, on slopes, along roads, near streams, and at the edges of woods in the foothills, montane, and subalpine ecosystems from Canada to New Mexico.

Comments: Also called Wood's Rose. Roses hybridize, so species may be hard to tell apart.

JAMES SAXIFRAGE
Telesonix jamesii
Saxifrage family (Saxifragaceae)

Description: Loose clusters of these bright pink to rose-purple flowers add a touch of color to boulder fields. The base of the reddish sepals forms a cup. The 5 petals look like they are attached to the rim. The petals have narrow bases and rounded tips. The kidney-shaped leaves are toothed. Stem leaves are small, and the stalked basal leaves usually are ½–2¼" wide. Reddish stems are covered with sticky hairs. This perennial grows 2–8" tall.

Midsummer.

Habitat/Range: Found in rocky or gravelly areas, it grows in rock cracks in the montane, subalpine, and alpine ecosystems from Canada to Colorado.

Comments: Also called Telesonix and Rock or Purple Saxifrage (*Saxifraga jamesii* or *Boykinia jamesii*).

James Saxifrage

H. WAYNE PHILLIPS

BEARDED SIDEBELLS PENSTEMON
Penstemon secundiflorus
Snapdragon family (Scrophulariaceae)

Description: Rose-pink, bluish purple, or dark purple flowers are arranged on one side of a smooth stem. The 2-lipped blossoms have 2 lobes above and 3 lobes below. The 5th, sterile, stamen has a thatch of yellow hairs (the "beard" of the common name). Flowers are up to 2" long. The thick, hairless leaves may have a whitish coating, making them look pale. The entire leaves are 1–4" long and clasp the stem. Plants grow 4–20" tall.

Spring to early summer.

Habitat/Range: Frequently seen on grassy slopes and gravelly or wooded sites in the foothills and montane ecosystems from Wyoming to New Mexico.

Comments: Also called Purple Beardtongue.

Bearded Sidebells Penstemon

Elephantella

ELEPHANTELLA
Pedicularis groenlandica
Snapdragon family (Scrophulariaceae)

Description: These unmistakable pinkish purple flowers look like miniature elephant heads. The petals resemble an elephant's head, ears, and long, curved trunk. The blossoms are arranged in a spike atop a purple stem. There are both basal and stem leaves. The leaves are fernlike—pinnately divided into leaflets with toothed lobes. Even the 2–10" long leaves have a purple color. The unbranched stems grow 6–28" high.

Midsummer.

Habitat/Range: Common in bogs, wet meadows, and near streams and ponds; found in the montane, subalpine, and alpine ecosystems from Alaska to New Mexico.

Comments: *Pedicularis* means "of lice." In Europe, farmers believed cattle feeding among these plants would become covered with lice. Also called Elephant Heads.

Rosy Paintbrush

ROSY PAINTBRUSH
Castilleja rhexifolia
Snapdragon family (Scrophulariaceae)

Description: The hairy sepals and bracts of this species are rose pink, purple, red, or occasionally, yellow. The bracts are entire or barely lobed, with the middle segment the largest. The inconspicuous petals are green, with the upper lip much longer than the lower lip. Relatively narrow leaves are 1–2½" long and have 3 main veins. The leaves mainly are entire, but the upper leaves may be 3 lobed. The unbranched stem grows 7–23" tall in clumps.
Mid- to late summer.

Habitat/Range: Common in moist meadows, open glades, and on hillsides in the subalpine and alpine ecosystems from Canada to Colorado.

Comments: Compare this species with Scarlet Paintbrush *(C. miniata).*

SHOWY VERVAIN
Glandularia bipinnatifida
Vervain family (Verbenaceae)

Description: Showy clusters of pink to purple flowers grow atop branched stems. The tubular, ¼–½" wide blossoms have 5 lobes that are notched at the tip. Below the flowers are bracts and sepals that often are sticky. Opposite, ¾–3" leaves usually are twice pinnately divided. The stems may be erect or the base may lie along the ground. The stems usually are hairy and grow 4–23" tall.
Early spring to midfall.

Habitat/Range: Found in fields and along roads in the foothills ecosystem from Utah and Colorado to Mexico. Also seen east to North Carolina and Florida.

Comments: Also called Rose Vervain or Western Pink Vervain *(Verbena ambrosifolia* or *V. canadensis).*

DENVER BOTANIC GARDENS

Showy Vervain

WHITE FLOWERS

*This section includes flowers that are
predominantly white. Since white flowers
grade into both pale pink and pale blue
flowers, and off-white flowers may appear
yellowish, readers should check the pink,
blue and purple, and yellow sections as well.*

Yucca

YUCCA
Yucca glauca
Agave family (Agavaceae)

Description: A raceme of creamy or greenish white, bell-shaped blossoms is borne on a woody stalk. The 1¼–2" long flowers have 6 thick, edible tepals, 6 stamens, and a green style. The narrow, pointed leaves look like light green daggers. The evergreen leaves usually are 10–33" long. Green, podlike fruits dry and split open to reveal round black seeds stacked like coins. The flowering stalks grow 1–5' high.

Late spring to early summer.

Habitat/Range: Found in dry fields and on sunny hillsides in the foothills ecosystem from Montana to New Mexico.

Comments: Also called Spanish Bayonet, Soapweed, or Plains Yucca. Formerly in the Lily family (Liliaceae). The blossoms open wide in the evening to facilitate pollination by the small pronuba moth *(Tegeticula yuccasella)*. The female moth pierces the ovary and lays an egg. She then collects a ball of yucca pollen and packs it into the stigma, insuring pollination. The pod produces many seeds, so there are some left after the moth larva has eaten its fill. Native Americans ate the young pods, made soap from the roots, and derived cordage from the leaf fibers.

DENVER BOTANIC GARDENS

Cutleaf Daisy

CUTLEAF DAISY
Erigeron compositus
Aster family (Asteraceae)

Description: This species usually has white, pink, or blue ray flowers and yellow disk flowers, but sometimes it lacks rays. The heads are ½–1" wide. The leaves are sticky, mainly basal, and divided 1–4 times into narrow, 3-lobed segments. Several stems grow in clumps with each stem carrying a single blossom. This perennial grows 2–10" high.

Late spring to midsummer.

Habitat/Range: Found in open pine forests, dry meadows, and gravelly areas in the foothills, montane, subalpine, and alpine ecosystems from Alaska to Arizona.

Comments: Also called Dwarf Mountain Fleabane or Gold Buttons (if it lacks ray flowers). People once believed if fleabane was burned, it would drive fleas and other insects away. As cattle overgraze an area, the numbers of this plant increase.

Mouse-Ear Chickweed

MOUSE-EAR CHICKWEED
Cerastium strictum
Chickweed family (Alsinaceae)

Description: Open clusters of white, ⅜–½" flowers grow atop weak stems. The 5 petals have a deep notch in the tip and the petals are at least twice as long as the 5 separate sepals. Bracts under the flower cluster have thin, dry edges. Narrow, opposite leaves are ⅜–1½" long and are covered with velvety hairs. The fruit is a cylindrical, seed-bearing capsule. This erect perennial often grows in clumps. The 2–12" stems may be sticky.

Early spring to late summer.

Habitat/Range: Found in dry meadows, open pine forests, and on slopes in the foothills, montane, subalpine, and alpine ecosystems from Canada to New Mexico.

Comments: Also known as Field Mouse-Ear or Meadow Chickweed *(C. arvense)*. Sometimes included in the Pink family (Caryophyllaceae). Alpine Mouse-Ear Chickweed *(C. beeringianum* ssp. *earlei)* has bracts with green edges.

COW PARSNIP
Heracleum sphondylium ssp. *montanum*
Parsley family (Apiaceae)

Description: Everything about this plant is huge, except its tiny white flowers. The blossoms are arranged in flat-topped clusters that may be up to 12" across. Petals are under ¼" long. The leaves are 6-16" long and look similar to maple leaves. They are palmately cleft or compound and typically have 3 toothed leaflets. The bases of the stem leaves have large sheaths. The small fruits are flat. The hollow, hairy stem can be more than ¾" in diameter and 2½–8' tall.

Late spring to late summer.

Habitat/Range: Found in wet meadows, open forests, and near streams in the foothills, montane, and subalpine ecosystems from Alaska to Arizona.

Comments: This genus is named after the mythical hero Hercules. The Blackfeet and other American Indians collected the stalks in spring and peeled, roasted, and ate them. Many members of this family are poisonous.

LORAINE YEATTS
Cow Parsnip

GIANT ANGELICA
Angelica ampla
Parsley family (Apiaceae)

Description: Tiny blossoms have white petals that turn greenish brown with age. The flowers are arranged in numerous round clusters 1" wide that make up a larger, globular cluster up to 6¼" across. Bractlets are narrow and inconspicuous. The leaves are twice pinnately compound with ovate, toothed leaflets. The fruit is narrowly winged. The stout, purplish stems are 3–7' tall and up to ¾" in diameter.

Mid- to late summer.

Habitat/Range: Found in shady sites, in moist meadows, and along streams in the foothills and montane ecosystems of Wyoming and Colorado.

Comments: The specific name *ampla* means "large."

ROCKY MOUNTAIN NATIONAL PARK

Giant Angelica

H. WAYNE PHILLIPS

Poison Hemlock

POISON HEMLOCK
Conium maculatum
Parsley family (Apiaceae)

Description: Clusters of small white flowers grow atop this tall, weedy plant. The twice compound, fernlike leaves are 6–12" long. The green, branched stems have purple spots. The seed-like fruits are ribbed. The smooth stems of this biennial plant grow 2–10' tall.

Mid- to late summer.

Habitat/Range: Found in moist disturbed sites of the foothills and montane ecosystems across North America, Eurasia, and Africa.

Comments: This plant is not native to North America. Ancient Greeks used juice from this poisonous plant to kill Socrates. Another poisonous member of this family is Water Hemlock *(Cicuta douglasii)*, which lacks the spotted stem and finely divided leaves.

LORAINE YEATTS

Porter Lovage

PORTER LOVAGE
Ligusticum porteri
Parsley family (Apiaceae)

Description: Flat clusters of white flowers grow atop this stout plant. Each blossom is less than ¼" across. The fernlike leaves are 6-12" long and pinnately compound with ovate leaflets. The small fruit is winged. The reddish, 18–42" stem is hollow and branched.

Mid- to late summer.

Habitat/Range: Common in meadows, wet areas, and aspen forests in the foothills, montane, and subalpine ecosystems from Wyoming to Mexico.

Comments: Also called Osha, Wild Parsnip, and Wild Celery. Wild populations are declining due to collectors digging up the medicinal roots. A similar species, Fernleaf Lovage *(L. tenuifolium)*, has narrow leaflets and a slender stem, and usually is under 20" tall.

ROCKY MOUNTAIN NATIONAL PARK

Blackheaded Daisy

BLACKHEADED DAISY
Erigeron melanocephalus
Aster family (Asteraceae)

Description: Typically, 50–70 white or pink-ish ray flowers surround yellow disk flowers. A solitary head 1½" across sits atop each stem. The bracts have woolly, black, or dark purple hairs. Basal leaves are spoon-shaped and up to 1½" long. Stem leaves are few and narrow. The hairy stems of this perennial are 2–6" tall.

Midsummer.

Habitat/Range: Common in moist meadows (such as those surrounding melting snowbanks) and on hillsides in the subalpine and alpine ecosystems of Wyoming, Utah, Colorado, and New Mexico.

Comments: In alpine areas, this plant may be confused with the bluish or lavender-flowered Alpine Fleabane *(E. simplex)*, which has bracts with lighter-colored hairs.

DENVER BOTANIC GARDENS

Colorado Thistle

COLORADO THISTLE
Cirsium scariosum
Aster family (Asteraceae)

Description: White to purplish disk flowers are arranged in heads that are ¾-2" wide and 1–1¾" tall. There typically are 1–8 heads per stem. The hairy bracts have spiny tips. The upper surfaces of the leaves lack spines. The edges of the alternate leaves have spiny teeth. This perennial may be stemless or have stout stems up to 4' high.

Early to late summer.

Habitat/Range: Found in moist meadows and aspen forests, on hillsides, and near streams in the montane and subalpine ecosystems from Colorado to Nevada and New Mexico.

Comments: Also called Elk Thistle *(C. coloradense* or *drummondii* var. *acaulescens).* The peeled stems and roots are edible.

LORAINE YEATTS

Rocky Mountain Pussytoes

ROCKY MOUNTAIN PUSSYTOES
Antennaria parvifolia
Aster family (Asteraceae)

Description: Flower heads that look like the pads of a cat's paw give this plant its common name. Usually, 3–8 heads containing only disk flowers are ¼" to just under ½" tall. The papery bracts around the flower heads have white or pinkish tips and a darkened base, but lack an obvious dark spot. Grayish, ¼–1" long leaves are primarily basal, with woolly hairs. The entire leaves are rounded at the tip and narrow toward the base. The vegetation spreads by leafy runners to form mats. Stems are 2–6" tall.

Early summer to early fall.

Habitat/Range: Common in dry meadows and open woods of the foothills, montane, and sub-alpine ecosystems from Canada to New Mexico.

Comments: Also called Sunloving Catspaw and Mountain, Nuttall's, or Small-Leaved Pussytoes. May be confused with the taller, leafy-stemmed Pearly Everlasting *(Anaphalis margaritacea).*

LORAINE YEATTS

Pearly Everlasting

PEARLY EVERLASTING
Anaphalis margaritacea
Aster family (Asteraceae)

Description: This plant looks like an oversized, leafy Pussytoes *(Antennaria)*. Clusters of ¼" wide flower heads have small yellow disk flowers surrounded by numerous white bracts. Ray flowers are lacking. The stems and undersides of the leaves have whitish, woolly hairs. Narrow, 1–5" long leaves are alternate, entire, and stalkless. This perennial is 9–36" tall.

Early summer to early fall.

Habitat/Range: Found in open coniferous forests and burned sites, on hillsides, and along roads in the foothills, montane, and subalpine ecosystems from Canada to New Mexico.

Comments: Also called Strawflower. The dried blossoms are used in flower arrangements.

WHIPLASH DAISY
Erigeron flagellaris
Aster family (Asteraceae)

Description: From 50–100 white ray flowers surround a circle of yellow disk flowers. The undersides of the rays are pinkish, lavender, or bluish. Buds are pink and nodding. One ¾" wide blossom sits atop each stem. The bracts under the flowers have sticky hairs. The mainly basal, hairy leaves are up to 1½" long and entire. Hairs are pressed close to an erect, slender stem. Runners on the surface of the ground may take root. This plant grows 2–16" tall.

Late spring to early fall.

Habitat/Range: Common in meadows and on grassy hillsides in the foothills and montane— and occasionally subalpine—ecosystems from Canada to Arizona.

Comments: Also called Trailing or Running Fleabane. The specific name *flagellaris* means "whiplike," referring to the runners.

H. WAYNE PHILLIPS

Whiplash Daisy

Stemless Easter Daisy

STEMLESS EASTER DAISY
Townsendia exscapa
Aster family (Asteraceae)

Description: White or pinkish ray flowers and yellow disk flowers make up a head about 1" wide. Stemless flowers are clustered directly atop the basal leaves. The edges of the bracts are thin and dry. Narrow, ¼–2" long, grayish leaves have hairs pressed flat to the leaf surface. This perennial is only 1–2" tall.

Early to late spring.

Habitat/Range: Dry fields, hillsides, and Pinyon-Juniper woodlands in the foothills and montane ecosystems from Canada to Arizona.

Comments: Also called Easter Townsendia, formerly *T. sericea*. The genus name honors John Kirk Townsend, ornithologist on the 1834 Wyeth Expedition to Oregon. This is one of the earliest blooming flowers of the plains and foothills.

Miner's Candle

MINER'S CANDLE
Oreocarya virgata
Borage family (Boraginaceae)

Description: Small white flowers with 5 lobes look like forget-me-nots, which also are members of the Borage family. The blossoms, together with long, leafy bracts, are arranged along the hairy stem. The narrow, 1–4" long leaves are covered with stiff hairs. A single, 8–24" stem typically is unbranched.

Midsummer.

Habitat/Range: Found in dry fields and on slopes in the foothills and montane ecosystems of Wyoming and Colorado.

Comments: The generic name *Oreocarya* means "mountain nut," referring to the nutlike seeds. Its specific name, *virgata,* means "wandlike." Formerly known by the scientific name *Cryptantha virgata.*

BROOK CRESS
Cardamine cordifolia
Mustard family (Brassicaceae)

Description: White flowers ½–¾" long are arranged in round clusters. Like other mustards, the 4 petals are arranged in a cross shape. The simple, heart-shaped leaves are ¾–2" long, long-stalked, and have wavy edges. Slightly flattened seedpods are ¾–1½" long. This perennial grows 4–30" tall in clumps.

Early summer to early fall.

Habitat/Range: Found in moist meadows, wet forests, and near streams and springs in the montane and subalpine ecosystems from Montana to New Mexico.

Comments: Also called Bitter Cress or Heart-Leaved Bittercress.

Brook Cress

LORAINE YEATTS

Mountain Candytuft

MOUNTAIN CANDYTUFT
Noccaea montana
Mustard family (Brassicaceae)

Description: Small, white to lavender flowers appear in clusters atop smooth stems. The four petals are ¼" long and arranged in a cross shape. Smooth, alternate leaves clasp the stem. Ovate or spoon-shaped basal leaves are ½–2" long and may be toothed. Heart-shaped seedpods are less than ½" long. This perennial has one or more unbranched stems that grow 1–16" tall.

Early spring to late summer.

Habitat/Range: Common in forests and on hillsides in the foothills, montane, subalpine, and alpine ecosystems from Canada to New Mexico.

Comments: Also called Mountain Pennycress, formerly *Thlaspi coloradense,* this is one of the earliest flowering plants in the foothills.

Mariposa Lily

MARIPOSA LILY
Calochortus gunnisonii
Mariposa family (Calochortaceae)

Description: These beautiful flowers look like delicate wild tulips. The 3 petals are white to pale lavender with yellow hairs near the base. The blossoms are up to 2" across with 6 stamens, 3 light green sepals, and a 3-parted stigma. There usually are one to several flowers on each stem. The grasslike alternate and basal leaves are entire and have parallel veins. Unbranched stems are 10–20" tall.

Late spring to midsummer.

Habitat/Range: Found in meadows, open forests, and on hillsides in the foothills, montane, and subalpine ecosystems from Montana to New Mexico.

Comments: Sometimes also placed in the Lily family (Liliaceae). The Ute Indians told Mormon settlers in Utah about the plant's edible, rootlike corm.

BUSH CRANBERRY
Viburnum edule
Honeysuckle family (Caprifoliaceae)

Description: Clusters of white blossoms adorn this shrub. The 5-lobed flowers have 5 stamens and 5 sepals. Simple leaves are toothed and may have 3 lobes, giving them the appearance of maple leaves. The opposite leaves are 1½–4¾" long. Branches are smooth, with the new growth brown or grayish. The edible, roundish red fruits have pits like a cherry. This shrub grows 2–6½' tall.

Late spring to midsummer.

Habitat/Range: Found in forests and near streams in the foothills, montane, and subalpine ecosystems from Canada to Colorado.

Comments: Also called High Bush Cranberry, Squashberry, or Arrow Wood, formerly *V. pauciflorum*.

H. WAYNE PHILLIPS

Bush Cranberry

DENVER BOTANIC GARDENS

Redberry Elder

REDBERRY ELDER
Sambucus microbotrys
Honeysuckle family (Caprifoliaceae)

Description: Small white flowers are arranged in pyramidal clusters. The opposite, pinnately compound leaves have 5–7 toothed leaflets. The twigs are covered with warty bumps. The clusters of small red or orange-red berries tempt jellymakers. The shrubs grow 3–10' tall.

Late spring to midsummer.

Habitat/Range: Common in moist meadows and open forests, on hillsides, and near streams in the montane and subalpine ecosystems from Canada to Colorado.

Comments: Also called Red Elderberry (*S. racemosa, melanocarpa,* or *pubens*). The generic name *Sambucus* is a Greek word for a musical instrument; the stem's pith may be removed to make a whistle.

ROCKY MOUNTAIN NATIONAL PARK

Alpine Sandwort

ALPINE SANDWORT
Lidia obtusiloba
Pink family (Caryophyllaceae)

Description: White, ⅜" wide flowers look large compared to this plant's tiny, mosslike leaves. The 5 rounded petals are longer than the green sepals. The blossoms have 10 stamens and 3 styles. The mainly basal leaves are less than ¼" long. Clustered stems have woody bases and very short, sticky hairs. This mat-forming plant grows ⅜–2⅜" tall.

Midsummer to early fall.

Habitat/Range: Common in sandy, windy, or rocky alpine areas from Alaska to New Mexico.

Comments: Also known by the scientific names *Minuartia biflora* and *Arenaria obtusiloba.* Some botanists include sandworts in the Chickweed family (Alsinaceae).

ROCKY MOUNTAIN LOCO
Oxytropis sericea
Bean family (Fabaceae)

Description: White or cream-colored flowers usually have a purple spot on the pointy-tipped keel. The pea-like, ¾–1" long blossoms are arranged in clusters atop a leafless stalk. Leaves are 2–12" long and are covered with grayish hairs. The pinnately compound leaves have 11–21 leaflets. The leathery pods are up to 1" long. The plants usually grow 6–16" tall in clumps.

Late spring to early fall.

Habitat/Range: Found in fields and on hillsides in the foothills, montane, and subalpine ecosystems from Canada to New Mexico.

Comments: Also called White, Silverleaf, or Silky Loco. Pink flowers may indicate a hybrid with Lambert's Loco *(O. lambertii).*

Rocky Mountain Loco

Arctic Gentian

ARCTIC GENTIAN
Gentianodes algida
Gentian family (Gentianaceae)

Description: These creamy white to yellow-green, goblet-shaped flowers are some of the last bloomers to grace the alpine tundra. The 1–1¾" tall blossoms have 4–5 pointed lobes with blue or purple lines and spots. There are 1–3 flowers atop each stem. Narrow, entire leaves are 1–4" long. Some of the opposite, stalkless leaves clasp the stem. This perennial grows 2–8" tall.

Late summer.

Habitat/Range: Found in meadows and near streams in the subalpine and alpine ecosystems from Alaska to New Mexico.

Comments: Gentians also are found in Europe, Asia, and New Guinea. This species formerly was known by the scientific names *Gentiana romanzovii* or *G. frigida.*

H. WAYNE PHILLIPS

Richardson Geranium

RICHARDSON GERANIUM
Geranium richardsonii
Geranium family (Geraniaceae)

Description: Dark pink or purple veins stand out against 5 white or pinkish petals. The 1" wide blossoms have 10 stamens. Typically paired flower stalks are covered with sticky hairs. The long-stalked leaves are palmately lobed into 3–7 segments. This perennial often has just 1 stem, which is 1–3' high. The pointy fruit is 1" long.

Late spring to late summer.

Habitat/Range: Found in moist, shady meadows, in aspen groves, and near streams in the foothills, montane, and subalpine ecosystems from Canada to New Mexico.

Comments: Also called White Geranium or Cranesbill. The common and specific names honor the nineteenth-century Arctic explorer Dr. John Richardson.

CLIFF FENDLER BUSH
Fendlera rupicola
Hydrangea Family (Hydrangeaceae)

Description: The numerous large, fragrant flowers have petals with a narrow stalked base. The petals are white, tinged with purple, and as long as ¾". Each flower has 8 stamens with broad, petal-like filaments that fork into 2 lobes near the anthers. These showy shrubs, 3-6' tall, sometimes are mistaken for mock oranges (*Philadelphus* species), which are distinguished by having numerous stamens with round filaments.

Midspring to early summer.

Habitat/Range: Found on rocky hillsides in oak and pine woodlands of the foothills and montane ecosystems from Colorado and Utah to New Mexico.

Comments: These shrubs are a favorite browse for deer. —*H. Wayne Phillips*

Cliff Fendler Bush

Fendler Waterleaf

FENDLER WATERLEAF
Hydrophyllum fendleri
Waterleaf family (Hydrophyllaceae)

Description: White or violet flowers with 5 rounded lobes are arranged in loose clusters. The 5 stamens stick out from the ¼–⅜" wide blossoms. Sepals are covered with bristly hairs. The 2¼–12" long leaves are pinnately divided into 5–13 segments with toothed edges. Stems have hairs that point downwards. This plant grows 8–36" tall.

Late spring to late summer.

Habitat/Range: Found in moist, shady sites— along streams, for example—in the foothills and montane ecosystems from Wyoming to New Mexico.

Comments: The similar, but shorter, Ball-Head Waterleaf *(H. capitatum)* has blue or lavender flowers in tight, round clusters.

ROCKY MOUNTAIN NATIONAL PARK

Alplily

ALPLILY
Lloydia serotina
Lily family (Liliaceae)

Description: Dainty blossoms have 6 separate, white tepals with purple veins. There usually is one erect or nodding flower per stem. The blossoms are ½–¾" wide and bear 6 stamens. The basal leaves are 2–6" long and very slender. Alternate stem leaves are much smaller. The fruit is a 3-parted capsule. The slender stems grow 2–6" tall.

Early to midsummer.

Habitat/Range: Found in rocky meadows and on ridges in the upper subalpine and alpine ecosystems from Alaska to New Mexico.

Comments: Also called Alpine Lily. The generic name honors British botanist Edward Lloyd.

FALSE SOLOMON'S SEAL
Maianthemum amplexicaule
Lily family (Liliaceae)

Description: Many tiny white flowers are arranged in dense clusters at the end of leafy stalks. The blossoms have 6 stamens that are longer than the 6 tepals. Alternate leaves are 2½–8" long. The ovate leaves may clasp the stem or have short stalks. The fruit is a red berry. The unbranched stems grow 1–3' high and often are found in groups.

Early spring to midsummer.

Habitat/Range: Found in moist forests in the foothills, montane, and subalpine ecosystems from Canada to Arizona.

Comments: Also called Wild Lily of the Valley and Claspleaf Solomonplume, formerly *Smilacina racemosa*. Some botanists place this plant in the Mayflower family (Convallariaceae). See description for the similar-looking Star Solomonplume.

H. WAYNE PHILLIPS

False Solomon's Seal

MOUNTAIN DEATH CAMAS
Anticlea elegans
Lily Family (Liliaceae)

Description: As its common name implies, this elegant flower is poisonous. The ½–¾" wide blossoms are borne in racemes. Each flower has 6 whitish tepals with yellowish green glands at the base and 6 stamens. The smooth, 6–12" long leaves look like wide blades of grass and may be slightly folded. Leaves appear mainly at the base of the stems. The unbranched stems grow 6–27" tall.

Early to late summer.

Habitat/Range: Found in grassy meadows and forests and near streams in the foothills, montane, subalpine, and alpine ecosystems from Alaska to New Mexico.

Comments: Also called Wand Lily. This plant used to be known by the generic name *Zigadenus.* Some botanists place this plant in the False Hellebore family (Melanthiaceae).

Mountain Death Camas

Sand Lily

SAND LILY
Leucocrinum montanum
Lily family (Liliaceae)

Description: Several star-shaped white blossoms sit among grasslike, basal leaves. The bases of the 6 tepals are fused to form a tube 1–3" long. The stemless flowers are 1–1¼" wide with 6 stamens topped by yellow pollen. The narrow basal leaves are 2–8" long.

Midspring to early summer.

Habitat/Range: Found in fields and open forests in the foothills and montane ecosystems from Montana to New Mexico.

Comments: Also called Mountain Lily or Star Lily. *Leucocrinum* is Greek for "white lily." According to William A. Weber and Ronald C. Wittmann (in *Colorado Flora: Eastern Slope*), the plant's ovary is underground. It elongates when mature, putting the seeds just beneath the soil surface. The next year's flower buds push up the previous season's ovary, scattering the seeds.

H. WAYNE PHILLIPS

Star Solomonplume

STAR SOLOMONPLUME
Maianthemum stellatum
Lily family (Liliaceae)

Description: Usually, 3–20 small, star-shaped blossoms are clustered at the end of a leafy stem. The ¼" wide flowers have 6 white tepals. Alternate, lance-shaped leaves are up to 6" long. The stalkless, partially folded leaves have pointy tips. Berries are green with dark stripes or are deep purple. Erect or somewhat downcurved stems are 8–24" tall and often grow in groups.

Midspring to midsummer.

Habitat/Range: Found in forests and meadows and near streams in the foothills, montane, and subalpine ecosystems from Canada to Texas.

Comments: Also called Starflower, Star Solomon's Seal, Wild Lily of the Valley, or False Solomon's Seal, formerly *Smilacina stellata.* Some botanists put this plant in the Mayflower family (Convallariaceae). See descriptions for the similar-looking False Solomon's Seal.

ROCKY MOUNTAIN NATIONAL PARK

Cutleaf Evening Primrose

CUTLEAF EVENING PRIMROSE
Oenothera coronopifolia
Evening Primrose family (Onagraceae)

Description: These flowers look like a smaller version of the blossoms of the Stemless Evening Primrose *(Oenothera caespitosa* ssp. *macroglottis)*. Like its relative, the Cutleaf Evening Primrose has 4 petals, a 4-parted stigma, and 8 stamens. The white, ½–1¼" wide flowers appear where the upper leaves meet the stem. The blossoms turn a pinkish color as they age. Short stem leaves are toothed or pinnately divided into narrow lobes. The hairy, branched, or simple stems of this perennial are 2–12" tall.

Late spring to late summer.

Habitat/Range: Found in meadows and along roads in the foothills and montane ecosystems from Wyoming to New Mexico.

Comments: The white blossoms stand out at night, making it easier for their moth pollinators to find them. Many flowers in this genus are pollinated by sphinx moths (Sphingidae family).

Stemless Evening Primrose

STEMLESS EVENING PRIMROSE
Oenothera caespitosa ssp. *macroglottis*
Evening Primrose family (Onagraceae)

Description: These huge white flowers are low to the ground. The showy blossoms are 2–4" across and fragrant. The 4 petals have slight indentations in the tip and the 4 hairy sepals are bent down. The 4-parted stigma is obvious and there are 8 stamens. The flowers are stemless but have a 2–4" long floral tube that may resemble a stem. Fleshy basal leaves usually are toothed and 1–6" long with winged stalks. The lance- or spoon-shaped leaves usually have finely hairy, wavy edges.

Late spring to late summer.

Habitat/Range: Found on gravelly hillsides and along roads and trails in the foothills, montane, and subalpine ecosystems from Canada to New Mexico.

Comments: Sometimes called Birdcage Evening Primrose. The flowers usually bloom from the late afternoon until the morning. The blossoms then turn pink and close.

LADY'S TRESSES
Spiranthes romanzoffiana
Orchid family (Orchidaceae)

Description: Numerous white flowers are arranged in 1–4 vertical rows that gently spiral up the top of the stem. These ¼–½" long blossoms lack a spur. The alternate, mainly basal leaves are lance-shaped and 2–10" long. These perennial plants grow 6–18" tall.

Midsummer to early fall.

Habitat/Range: Found in moist meadows, open woods, and along streamsides in the foothills, montane, and subalpine ecosystems from Alaska to New Mexico.

Comments: Also called Hooded Ladies' Tresses. Compare to White Bog Orchid *(Limnorchis dilatata* ssp. *albiflora),* which looks similar. The generic name *Spiranthes* means "spiral flower."

Lady's Tresses

Rattlesnake Plantain

RATTLESNAKE PLANTAIN
Goodyera oblongifolia
Orchid family (Orchidaceae)

Description: Rattlesnake Plantain is known more for its striking leaves than for its inconspicuous blossoms. The flowers are ¼–⅜" long, greenish white, and arranged in a loosely spiraled spike. Dark green, leathery leaves typically bear eye-catching white, reticulated markings. The simple basal leaves are 2–4" long with pointy tips. Soft, short hairs cover the stem, which grows 4–15½" tall.

Mid- to late summer.

Habitat/Range: Occasionally found in dry forests in the foothills, montane, and subalpine ecosystems from Alaska to New Mexico.

Comments: A similar species, *G. repens* ssp. *ophioides,* has shorter leaves that are ¼–1¼" long. The generic name honors John Goodyer, a seventeenth-century English naturalist. The common name refers to the leaves, which bear markings that look like a rattlesnake's skin.

White Bog Orchid

WHITE BOG ORCHID
Limnorchis dilatata ssp. *albiflora*
Orchid family (Orchidaceae)

Description: Small, fragrant white flowers and light green bracts are clustered atop a leafy stem. The blossom's hood is made up of 1 sepal and 2 petals. Another 2 sepals spread outwards to the sides. The lower petal is a tonguelike lip with a spur in the back. Alternate, lance-shaped leaves clasp the stem. Most of the 1½–8" long leaves appear at the base of a 4–24" unbranched stem.
Early summer to early fall.

Habitat/Range: Found in bogs, near streamsides, and in other wet areas of the montane, subalpine, and alpine ecosystems from Alaska to New Mexico.

Comments: Also called Bog Rein Orchid or Bog Candle, formerly *Habenaria dilatata*. Compare this flower to the similar-looking Lady's Tresses *(Spiranthes romanzoffiana)*.

ALPINE BISTORT
Bistorta vivipara
Buckwheat family (Polygonaceae)

Description: This smaller relative of American Bistort *(Bistorta bistortoides)* has a slender flower head that is ³⁄₁₆–¼" wide and 1–4" long. Below the white or pinkish flowers are small, dark bulblets that fall off and make new plants. Stalked basal leaves are ¾–3½" long. The alternate, stalkless stem leaves, smaller and narrower than the lower leaves, may clasp the stem and often have edges that are rolled downwards. This unbranched plant grows 4–12" tall.
Early to late summer.

Habitat/Range: Found in moist meadows and near streams in the subalpine and alpine ecosystems from Alaska to New Mexico.

Comments: Also called Serpentgrass, formerly *Polygonum viviparum*.

Alpine Bistort

AMERICAN BISTORT
Bistorta bistortoides
Buckwheat family (Polygonaceae)

Description: Tiny white or pinkish flowers are arranged in a tight, oblong cluster atop a tall, slender stem. The blossoms have 5 petal-like sepals and protruding stamens. The flower heads are 1–2⅜" long and ⅜–¾" wide. The mainly basal leaves are stalked and 4–10" long. The stem leaves are narrow, smaller, and un-stalked. The unbranched stem grows 8–27" tall.

Late spring to late summer.

Habitat/Range: Common in moist meadows and near streams in the montane, subalpine, and alpine ecosystems from Canada to New Mexico.

Comments: Also called Western Bistort, formerly *Polygonum bistortoides*. The roots are edible and best if roasted. The similar-looking Snowball Saxifrage *(Micranthes rhomboidea)* typically has flowers in a round cluster and fleshy basal leaves.

American Bistort

STAR PYROLA
Moneses uniflora
Wintergreen family (Pyrolaceae)

Description: One nodding, fragrant, white or sometimes pink flower grows atop a leafless stem. Each waxy blossom is ¾–1" across and usually has 5 petals, 10 stamens, and a straight style topped by a 5-parted stigma. Roundish, evergreen leaves are ½–1" long. The basal leaves have rounded teeth. This smooth plant may grow 2–5" tall.

Early to late summer.

Habitat/Range: Found in moist, shady coniferous forests and near streams in the montane and subalpine ecosystems from Alaska to New Mexico.

Comments: Also called One-Flowered Wintergreen, Single Delight, Wood Nymph, or Waxflower, formerly *Pyrola uniflora*. Pyrolas used to be in the Heath family (Ericaceae).

H. WAYNE PHILLIPS

Star Pyrola

ROCKY MOUNTAIN NATIONAL PARK

Alpine Spring Beauty

ALPINE SPRING BEAUTY
Claytonia megarhiza
Purslane family (Portulacaceae)

Description: Flowers with 5 white or pink petals with reddish veins often form a circle around a rosette of fleshy leaves. The ¾" wide blossoms have 2 sepals and 5 stamens. The 1–8" long basal leaves are thick and smooth. The spoon-shaped leaves may be edged in red. This low plant only grows to 5" tall.

Early to late summer.

Habitat/Range: Found on gravelly slopes and in rocky areas of the alpine tundra from Montana to New Mexico.

Comments: Also called Big-Rooted Spring Beauty because of its thick, long taproot. The root and succulent leaves help the plant collect and retain water in the tundra's drying winds.

BANEBERRY
Actaea rubra ssp. *arguta*
Buttercup family (Ranunculaceae)

Description: Tight clusters of small white flowers have many stamens. The 3–5 sepals and 4 or more petals soon drop off. The few large leaves are pinnately compound, typically 3 times, into toothed leaflets. The shiny red or white berries are about ¼" long and poisonous. This branched perennial usually grows 1–3' tall.

Late spring to midsummer.

Habitat/Range: Found in moist, shady forests and along streams in the foothills, montane, and subalpine ecosystems from Alaska to New Mexico.

Comments: The word "bane" is derived from a German word for "death." Also called Snakeberry or Chinaberry *(A. arguta).* Some botanists place Baneberry in the Hellebore family (Helleboraceae).

ROCKY MOUNTAIN NATIONAL PARK

Baneberry

Globeflower

GLOBEFLOWER
Trollius albiflorus
Buttercup family (Ranunculaceae)

Description: The blossom of this plant has several cream-colored or whitish, petal-like sepals that are oval-shaped. Usually, 1 flower sits atop each leafy stem. The 1–1½" wide blossoms have inconspicuous petals and numerous stamens. Alternate and basal leaves are palmately lobed and toothed. The smooth stems of this perennial grow 4–23" tall in groups.

Late spring to late summer.

Habitat/Range: Found in wet or moist sites in the montane, subalpine, and alpine ecosystems from Canada to Colorado.

Comments: Also called American Globeflower *(T. laxus).* Some botanists place Globeflower in the Hellebore family (Helleboraceae). Looks similar to Marsh Marigold *(Psychrophila leptosepala),* which has unlobed leaves.

Marsh Marigold

MARSH MARIGOLD
Psychrophila leptosepala
Buttercup family (Ranunculaceae)

Description: A single blossom grows atop each thick, leafless stem. The upper surfaces of the 5–15 petal-like sepals are white and the bottom surfaces are bluish. The flowers typically are 1–2" across with numerous yellow stamens. The mainly basal leaves are smooth and 3–8" long. The edges are entire or have rounded teeth. This plant grows 1–8" tall, often in clumps.

Late spring to late summer.

Habitat/Range: Commonly found in wet sites, especially near melting snowbanks, in the subalpine and alpine ecosystems from Canada to New Mexico.

Comments: Also called Elk's Lip Marsh Marigold *(Caltha leptosepala* or *rotundifolia).* Some botanists place Marsh Marigold in the Hellebore family (Helleboraceae). Moose and elk eat the leaves of this plant.

NARCISSUS ANEMONE
Anemonastrum narcissiflorum ssp. *zephyrum*
Buttercup family (Ranunculaceae)

Description: From 1–4 flowers usually sit atop each stout stem. There are 4–20 cream-colored or yellowish, petal-like sepals and numerous stamens. The sepals are ⅜–⅝" long. The leaves are mainly basal and palmately divided into deep, narrow lobes. Whorled or opposite stem leaves are stalkless. The stems of this 4–16" perennial have long hairs.

Midsummer.

Habitat/Range: Found in moist meadows of the subalpine and alpine ecosystems from Alaska to Colorado.

Comments: Also called Alpine Anemone, formerly *Anemone narcissiflora* or *A. zephyra.*

Narcissus Anemone

BOULDER RASPBERRY
Oreobatus deliciosus
Rose family (Rosaceae)

Description: This woody shrub has many showy white blossoms that are 1–3" wide. With 5 petals and many stamens, the solitary flowers look similar to those of the Wild Rose. The alternate, 1–2⅜" wide leaves have 3–5 shallow, rounded lobes with small teeth. The branches lack spines and have light brown bark that splits into flakes on the older growth. The fruit looks like a raspberry but is dry and seedy. This shrub grows 2–5' tall.

Late spring to early summer.

Habitat/Range: Found on dry hillsides and in rocky areas of the foothills and montane ecosystems of Wyoming and Colorado.

Comments: Formerly known by the scientific name *Rubus deliciosus.* Thimbleberry *(Rubacer* or *Rubus parviflorum)* looks similar but has larger leaves with pointed lobes.

Boulder Raspberry

Chokecherry

CHOKECHERRY
Padus virginiana ssp. *melanocarpa*
Rose family (Rosaceae)

Description: Small, sweet-smelling blossoms are arranged in cylindrical clusters on this shrub. The flowers have 5 petals and many stamens. Alternate, oval leaves 1½–5" long have pointy tips. The simple leaves bear small teeth along the edges. The smooth, brownish twigs lack thorns. The round fruits are ⅜" across with a cherrylike pit. The reddish purple to black cherries are edible, but sour. This subspecies usually grows 8–12' tall, but some varieties may be 2–32' high.

Midspring to midsummer.

Habitat/Range: Found in valleys, near streams, along fences, and on hillsides in the foothills and montane ecosystems from Canada to New Mexico.

Comments: Formerly known by the scientific name *Prunus melanocarpa.*

Mountain Dryad

MOUNTAIN DRYAD
Dryas octopetala ssp. *hookeriana*
Rose family (Rosaceae)

Description: Creamy white blossoms usually have 8 petals, hence its specific name, *octopetala*. The flowers typically are 1" wide with 8 sepals and many stamens. Leathery leaves are ¼–1½" long with small, rounded teeth. The edges often are rolled under and the leaves have white hairs on the lower surface. The numerous seeds have long, plumed tails. The woody stems hug the ground and often produce large mats of vegetation. The leafless, hairy flower stalk may be 1¼–8" high.

Mid- to late summer.

Habitat/Range: Common on gravelly slopes and windy ridges of the alpine tundra from Alaska to Colorado.

Comments: Also called White Mountain Avens. The name "dryad" refers to wood nymphs, the tiny fairylike creatures who live in oak forests. The plant gets this name because of its miniature oaklike leaves.

SERVICEBERRY
Amelanchier alnifolia
Rose family (Rosaceae)

Description: This shrub bears numerous clusters of white blossoms 1–2" wide. The fragrant flowers have 5 narrow petals and many stamens. Twigs and leaves are hairy when young and become smooth as they mature. The alternate, ¾–2" long leaves are oval or roundish and toothed at the upper end. The dark, bluish purple fruit is edible. This spineless shrub grows 3–22' tall.

Late spring to early summer.

Habitat/Range: Found on slopes, in open forests, and near streams in the foothills, montane, and subalpine ecosystems from Alaska to New Mexico.

Comments: Also called Shadbush and Alder-leaf Juneberry. Native Americans ate the berries raw or dried them for use as a winter food.

Serviceberry

WILD STRAWBERRY
Fragaria virginiana ssp. *glauca*
Rose family (Rosaceae)

Description: The 5-petaled white flowers are 1" wide with 5 sepals and many stamens. Palmately compound leaves have 3 toothed leaflets. The leaves are smooth, bluish, and have a coating that rubs off; they usually are taller than the hairy flowering stalks. The tooth at the end of the leaflet is shorter than the teeth next to it. The plants bear small red strawberries that are very flavorful. The 4" plants have red runners.

Midspring to late summer.

Habitat/Range: Found in meadows, moist forests, and on hillsides in the foothills, montane, and sub-alpine ecosystems from Canada to New Mexico.

Comments: Formerly called *Fragaria ovalis*. The flowers of Woodland Strawberry *(F. vesca* ssp. *bracteata,* formerly *F. americana)* are taller than the leaves. In addition, its leaves are hairy and the tooth at the end of the leaflet usually is longer than the teeth next to it.

Wild Strawberry

NORTHERN BEDSTRAW
Galium septentrionale
Madder family (Rubiaceae)

Description: Many tiny, 4-petaled flowers are arranged in clusters. The ⅛" wide blossoms have 4 stamens and no sepals. There are 4 leaves in each whorl. The narrow leaves are ¾–2" long with 3 obvious veins. The square stems are erect and usually lack hairs. This perennial grows 8–30" tall.

Late spring to late summer.

Habitat/Range: Common in meadows, in open forests, on hillsides, and near roads in the foothills, montane, and subalpine ecosystems from Alaska to New Mexico.

Comments: Also called Cleavers, formerly *G. boreale*. The dried plants were used to stuff mattresses, hence the common name Bedstraw. The generic name *Galium* is the Greek word for "milk"; a related species was used to curdle milk in order to make cheese. One of the plants that produces coffee beans, *Coffea arabica,* is in this family.

ROBERT TATINA
Northern Bedstraw

ROCKY MOUNTAIN NATIONAL PARK

Dotted Saxifrage

DOTTED SAXIFRAGE
Ciliaria austromontana
Saxifrage family (Saxifragaceae)

Description: It takes a close look to appreciate the delicate beauty of these small white flowers. Careful inspection reveals tiny orange and red spots on the petals. Several ⅜" wide flowers are borne on slender, reddish stalks that have small, alternate leaves. The flowers have 5 sepals and 10 stamens. Mosslike basal leaves have hairs on their edges and a spine at the tip. The leaves are ¼–¾" long. This perennial grows 2–6" tall and often forms mats of vegetation.

Early to late summer.

Habitat/Range: Found on and among rocks and in coniferous forests of the foothills, montane, subalpine, and alpine ecosystems from Canada to New Mexico.

Comments: Also called Spotted Saxifrage, formerly *Saxifraga bronchialis*. Saxifrage means "rock breaker"; the plants often grow in rock crevices.

SNOWBALL SAXIFRAGE
Micranthes rhomboidea
Saxifrage family (Saxifragaceae)

Description: Small white flowers are clustered in a round head atop a leafless stalk. The blossoms have 5 petals, 5 sepals, and 10 stamens. Fleshy, ¾–3" long leaves are arranged in a basal rosette. The ovate or diamond-shaped leaves are smooth, the edges usually toothed, and the leaves have short, wide stalks. The 2–12" flowering stem is covered with sticky hairs.

Late spring to late summer.

Habitat/Range: Found in meadows and rocky areas in the foothills, montane, subalpine, and alpine ecosystems from Canada to Colorado.

Comments: Also called Diamond-Leaf Saxifrage, formerly *Saxifraga rhomboidea*. This plant may be confused with American Bistort *(Bistorta bistortoides)*, which has alternate and basal leaves that are long and narrow.

ROCKY MOUNTAIN NATIONAL PARK

Snowball Saxifrage

PARRY LOUSEWORT
Pedicularis parryi
Snapdragon family (Scrophulariaceae)

Description: A cluster of creamy white, yellowish, or pinkish flowers adorns the top of smooth stems. The pointed upper lip of the flower looks somewhat like the head of a goose. The blossoms are ½–1" long and interspersed with green bracts. The mainly basal leaves are deeply pinnately divided and 2–4¾" long. Stem leaves are smaller. This plant often grows in clusters 4–16" tall.

Midsummer.

Habitat/Range: Common in meadows and on gravelly slopes in the subalpine and alpine ecosystems from Montana to New Mexico.

Comments: This plant may be confused with Canada Lousewort *(P. canadensis* ssp. *fluviatilis)*, whose leaves are not as deeply divided. Canada Lousewort usually is found in the foothills and montane ecosystems.

Parry Lousewort

Snowlover

SNOWLOVER
Chionophila jamesii
Snapdragon family (Scrophulariaceae)

Description: Cream-colored or greenish white, tubular flowers usually are clustered on one side of the stem. The ⅜–¾" long blossoms are 2-lipped, with 2 lobes above and 3 below. The flowers have 5 stamens, the 5th one sterile. Leaves are mainly basal, spoon-shaped, fleshy, and entire. Stem leaves are smaller and narrower. This perennial grows 2–4" tall.

Midsummer.

Habitat/Range: Found in moist, gravelly areas and near melting snowbanks on the alpine tundra of Wyoming and Colorado.

Comments: Named for Edwin James, a botanist and the first documented white man to climb Pikes Peak. During that climb in 1820, James collected specimens of this plant.

ROCKY MOUNTAIN NATIONAL PARK

Twisted Stalk

TWISTED STALK
Streptopus fassettii
Bellwort family (Uvulariaceae)

Description: Greenish white to cream-colored, almost spider-shaped flowers dangle from bent stalks located where the leaves attach to the stem. The blossoms are about ⅜" long with 6 tepals that curve backward. Alternate, stalkless leaves clasp the stem. The ovate, 3–4" long leaves have parallel veins. The roundish berries are orange-red and smooth. The stems are arched, branched, and lack hairs. This plant grows 1–3½' tall.

Late spring to late summer.

Habitat/Range: Found in moist forests and near streams in the foothills, montane, and subalpine ecosystems from Alaska to New Mexico.

Comments: Also called Liverberry *(S. amplex-ifolius)*. Formerly in the Lily family (Liliaceae). The generic name means "twisted foot," referring to the bent flower stalks.

Canada Violet

CANADA VIOLET
Viola scopulorum
Violet family (Violaceae)

Description: Small, 5-petalled white flowers arise from the leaf axils. The back side of the blossoms are purple. The petals may be yellow at the bases or have purple lines. Heart-shaped leaves are ¾" wide and dark green. The leaves are entire or have finely toothed edges and a narrow tip. The leafy stems are 4-12" tall and usually smooth.

Late spring to midsummer.

Habitat/Range: Found on shady, moist hillsides and in canyons in the foothills, montane, and subalpine ecosystems from Colorado to New Mexico.

Comments: Rydberg Violet *(V. rydbergii)* has a hairy stem and hairs on the inner surface of the side petals. As its name implies, the stemless Kidneyleaf Violet *(V. renifolia* var. *brainerdii)* has kidney-shaped leaves. Swamp White Violet *(V. macloskey* ssp. *pallens)* also is stemless and grows in wet areas.

YELLOW FLOWERS

This section includes flowers ranging from bright golden yellow and yellow-orange to pale, creamy yellow. Since yellow flowers grade into red, pink, and white flowers, readers looking for yellow flowers should check the red and orange, pink, and white sections as well.

Mountain Parsley

MOUNTAIN PARSLEY
Pseudocymopterus montanus
Parsley family (Apiaceae)

Description: Tiny yellow flowers are grouped in flat-topped clusters up to 2" across. There is 1 main cluster per stem. Some of the green secondary bracts may extend past the edge of the flower cluster. There are a few smooth basal leaves with long stalks; these leaves are not stiff like those of Whiskbroom Parsley *(Harbouria trachypleura).* The leaves are pinnately divided. The lobes of the leaflets are about ⅛" wide and taper at each end. The small fruits are winged. The plants grow 8–31" in height.

Early to late summer.

Habitat/Range: Found in fields and aspen forests and on rocky hillsides in the foothills, montane, subalpine, and alpine ecosystems from Wyoming to Mexico.

Comments: Similar to Whiskbroom Parsley *(Harbouria trachypleura).*

WHISKBROOM PARSLEY
Harbouria trachypleura
Parsley family (Apiaceae)

Description: Clusters of tiny yellow flowers sit atop a long stalk. There usually are 1–3 main clusters per stem; each clump is about 2" across. The secondary bracts usually do not extend past the edge of the flower cluster. Numerous stiff basal leaves are divided 2 times into 3-lobed segments. The lobes of the leaflets typically are less than ¹⁄₁₆" wide and do not taper at both ends. Branching stems often grow in clumps 3–20" tall. The small fruits lack wings.

Late spring to midsummer.

Habitat/Range: Found in dry meadows, open coniferous forests, and on sunny slopes in the foothills and montane ecosystems from Wyoming to Mexico.

Comments: Very similar to Mountain Parsley *(Pseudocymopterus montanus).* Alpine Parsley *(Oreoxis alpina)* is a dwarf alpine plant up to 4" tall. On Pikes Peak, it is replaced by *O. humilis,* which grows nowhere else in the world.

Whiskbroom Parsley

ALPINE SUNFLOWER
Rydbergia grandiflora
Aster family (Asteraceae)

Description: These large yellow sunflowers look like giants compared to the other tiny tundra wildflowers. Each stem bears a single, nodding flower head 2–4½" wide. Woolly bracts protect the flower buds from harsh alpine weather. The mainly basal leaves are 3–4" long, hairy, and divided into slender segments. The stout, woolly stems are 1–12" tall.

Midsummer.

Habitat/Range: May be abundant on dry hillsides, in meadows, and on windy ridges on the alpine tundra from Montana to New Mexico.

Comments: Also called Old-Man-of-the-Mountain, Alpine Goldflower, Sun God, and Mountain Sunflower, formerly *Hymenoxys grandiflora*. The generic name is a tribute to the botanist Per Axel Rydberg, who studied the flora of the Rockies.

Alpine Sunflower

Annual Sunflower

ANNUAL SUNFLOWER
Helianthus annuus
Aster family (Asteraceae)

Description: Large sunflowers grow from the tall, leafy stems of this annual. Ray flowers are yellow with brownish or reddish purple disk flowers. Below the 3–5" wide heads are bracts rimmed by stiff hairs. Most leaves are alternate and rough. The lower leaves are 2–10" long, heart-shaped or ovate, and may be entire or toothed. Hairy stems are branched above and grow 1–13' in height.

Midsummer to early fall.

Habitat/Range: Abundant in fields, disturbed areas, and along roads in the foothills and montane ecosystems from Canada to New Mexico.

Comments: Also called Kansas Sunflower or Mirasol. According to Lewis and Clark, Native Americans who lived along the Missouri River used the seeds to thicken soup and as an ingredient in bread. This species hybridizes with the smaller Plains Sunflower *(H. petiolaris)*.

Aspen Sunflower

ASPEN SUNFLOWER
Helianthella quinquenervis
Aster family (Asteraceae)

Description: A single nodding head usually sits atop the stem, although there may be some smaller heads below. Heads have up to 20 light yellow ray flowers and deep yellow to reddish brown disk flowers. Below the 2–4" wide heads are bracts with hairy margins. Basal leaves are up to 19" long and lance-shaped. There typically are 4 pairs of opposite, leathery stem leaves. The leaves are prominently 5-veined. Clusters of unbranched stems grow 1–4½' in height.

Early to late summer.

Habitat/Range: Found in aspen forests, in meadows, and on hillsides in the foothills, montane, and subalpine ecosystems from Montana to Mexico.

Comments: Also called Nodding or Little Sunflower. The specific name *quinquenervis* refers to the 5 nerves in the ray flowers.

BALSAMROOT
Balsamorhiza sagittata
Aster family (Asteraceae)

Description: A single yellow, sunflower-like head usually sits atop a stout stalk. The flowering stalks bear only a handful of small leaves. Underneath 2¼–4½" wide blossoms are woolly bracts. The specific name means arrow-shaped, which aptly describes the leaves. Numerous 8–16" long, entire leaves are on long stalks, and they are covered with silvery, woolly hairs. This perennial grows 8–32" tall.

Late spring to midsummer.

Habitat/Range: Found in valleys, open forests, and on slopes in the foothills and montane ecosystems from Montana to Colorado. Hundreds of these plants may color fields and hillsides a brilliant yellow.

Comments: Also called Arrowleaf Balsamroot. Native Americans ate the young shoots and leaves as well as the roots and seeds. The root also was used as a poultice for wounds and brewed in a tea for treatment of colds and stomachaches.

Balsamroot

BLACK-EYED SUSAN
Rudbeckia hirta
Aster family (Asteraceae)

Description: A dome of dark brown to black disk flowers stands out against yellow or light orange ray flowers. The sunflower-like heads are up to 3" across. Lower leaves are lance-shaped while the upper leaves are narrower. Hairy, alternate leaves are up to 6" long. The simple leaves may be entire or have some shallow teeth. This perennial grows 1–30" in height.

Mid- to late summer.

Habitat/Range: Commonly found in meadows, aspen forests, on slopes, and near trails in the foothills and montane ecosystems from Canada to Texas.

Comments: This species from the eastern United States has spread widely in the West. The generic name honors Olaf Rudbeck, a seventeenth-century Swedish botany professor.

Black-Eyed Susan

Blacktip Senecio

BLACKTIP SENECIO
Senecio atratus
Aster family (Asteraceae)

Description: Yellow ray flowers and orange disk flowers are arranged in clusters atop a hairy stem. The flower heads have 3–5 rays and are ½" across. Under the flower heads are 8 black-tipped bracts with fuzzy bases. The stalked basal leaves are 4–8" long and oblong. Alternate, stalkless stem leaves are lance-shaped and smaller at the top of the stem. The woolly leaves are grayish green and often have tiny teeth. This stout perennial plant grows in clumps 12–31" tall.

Early to late summer.

Habitat/Range: Common on gravelly hillsides and along roads in the montane and subalpine ecosystems of Utah, Colorado, and New Mexico.

Comments: Some other senecios also have black-tipped bracts, but none of them have very hairy leaves and stems. Wooton Senecio *(S. wootonii)* has leaves with a whitish coating and a winged leaf stalk. Thickbract Senecio *(S. crassulus)* has stalkless upper stem leaves that clasp the stem.

Blanket Flower

BLANKET FLOWER
Gaillardia aristata
Aster family (Asteraceae)

Description: Resembling a red-eyed sunflower, this *Gaillardia* is one of the showiest blossoms of the Rockies. The yellow ray flowers have 3-lobed tips and their bases often are colored with red. Flower heads are up to 3½" across. Reddish purple disk flowers form a ball ¾–2¼" wide at the center of the flower head. The hairy, lance-shaped leaves are 2–8" long and may be entire or toothed. One or more hairy stems grow to 8–30" in height.

Mid- to late summer.

Habitat/Range: Found in meadows and on dry hillsides in the foothills and montane ecosystems from Canada to New Mexico.

Comments: Also called Brown-Eyed Susan or Indian Blanket. A similar species, Pinnate-Leaf Blanket Flower *(G. pinnatifida)*, is a perennial of the southern Rockies that has some leaves pinnately divided. Firewheel *(G. pulchella)* is an annual with reddish ray flowers tipped with yellow.

BUSH SUNFLOWER
Helianthus pumilus
Aster family (Asteraceae)

Description: As the common name implies, this short sunflower has a bushy appearance. Ray flowers are yellow with yellowish brown disk flowers. The heads are up to 3⅛" wide. Usually, 1–3 heads sit atop the stems. Most of the 1–4" long leaves are entire and opposite. The ovate or lance-shaped, dull green leaves have short stalks and stiff, short hairs. This perennial has several hairy stems and grows 12–31" in height.

Early to late summer.

Habitat/Range: Found in fields, in open forests, and on dry hillsides in the foothills and montane ecosystems in Wyoming and Colorado.

Comments: Also called Perennial or Dwarf Sunflower.

Bush Sunflower

Fringed Sagewort

FRINGED SAGEWORT
Artemesia frigida
Aster family (Asteraceae)

Description: Tiny yellow disk flowers are arranged in loose clusters atop leafy stems. The blossoms face out from the stem or may be slightly nodding. The leaves are deeply divided several times into short, very narrow segments; they are light green and covered in short, silvery hairs. Basal leaves appear in clumps; leaves along the stems are alternate. Branched stems are woody at the base. This hairy-stemmed perennial grows 4–16" tall.

Midsummer to early fall.

Habitat/Range: Common in meadows, open forests, on hillsides, and near roads and trails in the foothills, montane, and subalpine ecosystems from Canada to Arizona.

Comments: Also called Pasture Sagebrush, Mountain Sage, or Silver Sage. The silvery green foliage and pungent smell of the crushed leaves make the *Artemesias* easy to recognize. They are not related to cooking Sage *(Salvia officinalis)*, which is in the mint family.

ROCKY MOUNTAIN NATIONAL PARK

Goldenglow

GOLDENGLOW
Rudbeckia ampla
Aster family (Asteraceae)

Description: Yellow ray flowers 1–2" long droop from a cone-shaped mound of dull yellow or greenish brown disk flowers. The flower heads may be 3–5" across. The long-stalked lower leaves are divided into 3–7 toothed lobes that are 3–8" long. The alternate upper leaves are entire or 3-lobed. The branched stems grow 2–6½' tall.

Midsummer to midfall.

Habitat/Range: Common in moist meadows, aspen forests, and along streamsides in the foothills and montane ecosystems from Canada to New Mexico.

Comments: Also called Tall Coneflower and Cutleaf Coneflower. The domestic plant known as Goldenglow was derived from this wildflower.

GOLDEN RABBITBRUSH
Chrysothamnus nauseosus ssp. *graveolens*
Aster family (Asteraceae)

Description: This shrub is crowned with clusters of yellow blossoms. The ¼–⅜" long flower heads have only disk flowers with yellowish, smooth bracts. The alternate, entire leaves are very narrow. Some of the leaves, which are grayish, have 3–5 veins. Branched stems are light green and covered with woolly hairs. This perennial usually grows 2–5' tall.

Midsummer to midfall.

Habitat/Range: Found in fields, open forests, disturbed areas, and along roads in the foothills and montane ecosystems from Montana to New Mexico.

Comments: The generic name comes from Greek words meaning "gold bush." The specific name *nauseosus* means "nauseating"; *graveolens* means "heavy scented."

LORAINE YEATTS

Golden Rabbitbrush

ROCKY MOUNTAIN NATIONAL PARK

Hairy Golden Aster

HAIRY GOLDEN ASTER
Heterotheca villosa
Aster family (Asteraceae)

Description: Several flower heads ½–1" wide sit atop a branched, leafy stem. Both ray and disk flowers are yellow. The bracts below the flower head usually are leafy. The alternate leaves are lance-shaped or narrowly oblong and hairy. Lower leaves have stems while the upper leaves do not. The leaves are ½–2¾" long. The plants, which have more than one stem that is covered with short gray hairs, grow 8–23" tall. The seeds are crested with white bristles.

Early to late summer.

Habitat/Range: Common on hillsides, in open areas, and along roads in the foothills and montane ecosystems from Canada to Mexico.

Comments: Also called Goldeneye, formerly *Chrysopsis villosa*. The specific name *villosa* means "with soft hairs."

Heartleaf Arnica

HEARTLEAF ARNICA
Arnica cordifolia
Aster family (Asteraceae)

Description: From 9 to 13 yellow ray flowers usually surround yellow disk flowers in heads 2–3" wide or wider. Below the 1–3 heads are hairy bracts. As the specific name implies, the lower leaves are heart-shaped. The largest leaves are up to 5" long and are found on separate shoots. The opposite stem leaves are velvety. The upper leaves are ovate and without stalks. Hairy stems grow 4–24" tall.

Late spring to midsummer.

Habitat/Range: Found in coniferous or aspen forests of the foothills, montane, and subalpine ecosystems from Alaska to New Mexico.

Comments: Also called Leopard's Bane. Colonists used a tincture made from this plant externally for sprains and cuts. Some children who have ingested this plant have gone into comas. Arnicas today are used in some creams for sore muscles.

LAMBSTONGUE GROUNDSEL
Senecio integerrimus
Aster family (Asteraceae)

Description: Typically, 5–30 flower heads ¼–¾" wide grow atop hollow stems. The central flower head has a shorter flowering stalk than other nearby flower heads. Both ray flowers and disk flowers are yellow. The leaves have wavy margins or small teeth. The stem leaves are alternate and usually smaller than the thick basal leaves, which are 2¼–6" long. The top leaves clasp the stem. When young, the leaves and stems are covered with white, cobwebby hairs. The stout stems are 8–28" tall.

Midspring to midsummer.

Habitat/Range: Found in meadows, open forests, along roadsides, and on slopes in the foothills, montane, and subalpine ecosystems from Canada to Colorado.

Comments: Also called Common Spring Senecio, Butterweed, or Ragwort.

DENVER BOTANIC GARDENS

Lambstongue Groundsel

MOUNTAIN GUMWEED
Grindelia subalpina
Aster family (Asteraceae)

Description: The most prominent features of this yellow sunflower are the bracts with narrow, curved tips. The common name refers to the flower heads, which are sticky. Numerous heads may be more than 1" wide with yellow ray flowers and disk flowers. The simple, alternate leaves usually are 2–3" long. The thick, oblong leaves are mostly toothed, but the upper leaves may be entire. A leafy, branched stem grows 6–23" tall.

Midsummer to early fall.

Habitat/Range: Found in meadows, on disturbed ground, and on hillsides in the foothills, montane, and lower subalpine ecosystems of Wyoming and Colorado.

Comments: The Ponca and Dakota Indians treated tuberculosis and colic with gumweed. The Cheyenne treated skin sores with a tea made of the boiled flowers.

Mountain Gumweed

Orange Sneezeweed

ORANGE SNEEZEWEED
Helenium autumnale var. *montanum*
Aster family (Asteraceae)

Description: These large blossoms are a beautiful yellowish orange. The ray flowers hang down from a disk that looks like a flat-topped anthill. The blossoms are 2–3" across with rays that are toothed at the tip. There are several heads on each stem. The leaves are 5–12" long and get smaller and stalkless toward the top of the stem. Some of the leaf bases extend down the stem. The simple leaves are oblong or lance-shaped. This perennial grows 2–4' tall.

Midsummer to early fall.

Habitat/Range: Found in moist meadows, along streams, and near roads in the foothills, montane, and subalpine ecosystems from Montana to New Mexico.

Comments: The Comanches and other Native Americans inhaled the dried, powdered flowers to induce sneezing and clear out stuffy sinuses. The leaf bases of a similar species, *Dugaldia hoopesii*, do not extend down the stem.

Salsify

TRIANGULARLEAF SENECIO
Senecio triangularis
Aster family (Asteraceae)

Description: Eight yellow ray flowers surround yellow disk flowers in heads 1–1½" across. Like other senecios, the bracts below the flower head are the same length and in one row, except for a few shorter bracts at the bottom. Alternate, triangular leaves are 2–8" long. The leaves are coarsely toothed and mainly smooth. The stout, leafy stems usually are smooth. The plants grow in clumps 1–5' tall.

Early summer to early fall.

Habitat/Range: Abundant along streamsides and in moist open woods, swamps, and other wet areas in the montane and subalpine ecosystems from Alaska to New Mexico.

Comments: *Senecio* means "old man," referring to the hairy, white bristles attached to the seeds.

SALSIFY
Tragopogon dubius ssp. *major*
Aster family (Asteraceae)

Description: This dandelion look-alike has a single lemon-yellow flower head atop a stem 1–3' tall. The heads are 1–2" or more across and have only ray flowers. There usually are 10–13 green, pointed bracts that are longer than the ray flowers. Grasslike leaves 5–6" long clasp the stem. The hollow stems are branched below and have milky sap. Numerous seeds with little parachutes form a round seed head that is 2–4" in diameter.

Late spring to early fall.

Habitat/Range: Found in meadows and along roadsides in the foothills, montane, and lower subalpine ecosystems from Idaho to New Mexico. Also seen in the eastern United States.

Comments: A non-native originally from Europe. Also called Oyster Plant or Oyster Root. This species looks like Meadow Salsify *(T. pratensis)*, which has purple-margined bracts that are not longer than the ray flowers.

ROCKY MOUNTAIN NATIONAL PARK

Triangularleaf Senecio

ROCKY MOUNTAIN NATIONAL PARK

Creeping Hollygrape

CREEPING HOLLYGRAPE
Mahonia repens
Barberry family (Berberidaceae)

Description: Groups of small yellow flowers each have 6 petals, 6 petal-like sepals, and 6 stamens. The alternate, pinnately compound leaves have 3–7 evergreen leaflets, which are spiny, 3" long, and holly-like. The leathery leaflets often turn red in the fall. Plants grow to 10" tall. The dark blue to black berries are edible, but are best when sweetened.

Midspring to midsummer.

Habitat/Range: Found on dry slopes and in forests of the foothills and montane ecosystems from Canada to New Mexico.

Comments: Also called Oregon Grape, Mountain Holly, or Creeping Barberry. The specific name *repens* means "creeping," referring to the way the plant spreads from underground stems.

Narrowleaf Puccoon

NARROWLEAF PUCCOON
Lithospermum incisum
Borage family (Boraginaceae)

Description: Bright yellow, trumpet-shaped flowers are found where the upper leaves meet the stem. The 5-lobed petals have ruffled edges. The blossoms are ½–1¼" long. The narrow, alternate leaves are ½–2½" long with entire margins. The plants have several hairy, leafy stems that grow 4–18" tall.

Late spring to midsummer.

Habitat/Range: Found in dry meadows, open forests, and on hillsides in the foothills and montane ecosystems from Canada to New Mexico.

Comments: Also called Fringed Gromwell. *Lithospermum* means "stone seed," which refers to the 4 hard nutlets. The smaller blossoms of the related Many-Flowered Puccoon *(L. multiflorum)* lack the fringed lobes and usually bloom later. The name "puccoon" comes from an Algonquian word denoting plants that produce a yellow or red dye.

GOLDEN DRABA
Draba aurea
Mustard Family (Brassicaceae)

Description: Yellow, 4-petaled flowers have 4 hairy sepals and 6 stamens. Styles are 1⁄16" long or less. The small flowers are clustered at the top of leafy stems. Basal leaves are ¼–2" long and arranged in a rosette. The thick leaves are covered with fine hairs, are oval or spoon-shaped, and usually are entire. Seedpods are flattened and contorted, but usually not twisted. The fruits are up to ½" long. Plants usually are 3–19" tall and grow in clumps.

Midsummer.

Habitat/Range: Abundant in fields, dry pine forests, and on hillsides in the montane, subalpine, and alpine ecosystems from Alaska to New Mexico.

Comments: The taller Spectacular or Showy Draba *(D. spectabilis)* has toothed leaves.

Golden Draba

TWISTED-FRUIT DRABA
Draba streptocarpa
Mustard Family (Brassicaceae)

Description: From 10–60 yellow flowers are arranged in clusters. The cross-shaped flowers have 4 yellow petals about ¼" long and 4 hairy sepals. Some of the styles are longer than ¹⁄₁₆". Basal leaves have coarse hairs and are ¼–1⅜" long. The leaves usually are entire. The hairy stem may be twisted. Seedpods are hairy and twisted. This perennial grows ¾–12" tall.

Early to late summer.

Habitat/Range: Found in fields, forest clearings, and on gravelly hillsides of the montane, subalpine, and alpine ecosystems in Colorado and New Mexico.

Comments: The specific name *streptocarpa* means "twisted-fruit."

Twisted-Fruit Draba

Western Wallflower

WESTERN WALLFLOWER
Erysimum capitatum
Mustard family (Brassicaceae)

Description: Fragrant flowers in a showy, ball-like cluster typically are yellow, orange, or maroon (sometimes lavender or brownish). The 4 petals are more than ¼" long, with the blossoms ¾" wide. Narrow, 1–5" long leaves are basal or alternate, covered with rough hairs, and usually have small teeth. The slender, 2–4" long pods have 4 sides. The plants grow 6–36" in height with few or no branches.

Midspring to midsummer.

Habitat/Range: Found in meadows, pine forests, and on gravelly hillsides in the foothills, montane, subalpine, and alpine ecosystems from Canada to New Mexico.

Comments: Also called Prairie Rocket, formerly *E. nivale* or *E. asperum.* A similar montane species, Treacle Wallflower or Wormseed Mustard *(E. cheiranthoides* ssp. *altum)*, has yellow flowers with shorter petals and bears a fruit less than 1¼" long.

ROCKY MOUNTAIN NATIONAL PARK

Plains Prickly Pear

PLAINS PRICKLY PEAR
Opuntia polyacantha
Cactus family (Cactaceae)

Description: Large, showy flowers commonly are yellow but may be pink; the flowers fade to a copper color. The 2–3" wide blossoms have many shiny petals and numerous stamens. Flowers are borne at the edge of the pads. The jointed, oval stems are flattened into pads 2–6" long; these are spiny but not wrinkled. There are 3–10 spines per cluster; the rigid spines are 2–3" long. The pads also bear small bristles. The edible, oval fruit is ¾–1½" long, spiny, and tan. These spreading plants are 3–6" tall.

Late spring to midsummer.

Habitat/Range: Grows in dry, sunny areas of the foothills ecosystem from Canada to New Mexico.

Comments: Also called Hunger or Starvation Cactus because its dry fruits were a last-chance food choice. The fleshy fruits of Prickly Pear Cactus *(O. macrorhiza)* were preferred. Fragile Prickly Pear *(O. fragilis)* has rounder stems. Members of several Great Plains Indian nations used the mucilaginous juice of Prickly Pears to waterproof and preserve painted designs on leather.

YELLOW STONECROP
Amerosedum lanceolatum
Stonecrop family (Crassulaceae)

Description: Clusters of yellow, star-shaped flowers sit atop fleshy stems. The blossoms are ¼–½" wide with 4–5 pointed petals, 4–5 sepals, and 8–10 stamens. Narrow, succulent leaves form tight basal rosettes. The green or reddish brown leaves are ¼–¾" long. The alternate, unstalked stem leaves are smooth with a waxy coating to retain moisture. This perennial grows 4–8" tall.

Early to late summer.

Habitat/Range: Common on dry, rocky sites in the foothills, montane, subalpine, and alpine ecosystems from Canada to New Mexico.

Comments: Also called Orpine, formerly *Sedum stenopetalum.* The young flowers, leaves, and stems are edible raw.

Yellow Stonecrop

GOLDEN BANNER
Thermopsis divaricarpa
Bean family (Fabaceae)

Description: The showy racemes of these large, yellow, pea-like flowers are hard to miss. The blossoms have 5 petals and 10 separate filaments. Palmately compound leaves have 3 leaflets that are 1–2⅜" long. Leaflike stipules are found where the leaves join the stem. Seedpods are slightly curved or straight, somewhat hairy, and stick out perpendicularly from the stem. The plants, 1–2' tall, often grow in groups.

Late spring to early summer.

Habitat/Range: Common on hillsides, in meadows, near streams, or in partial shade in the foothills, montane, and subalpine ecosystems from Wyoming to New Mexico

Comments: False Lupine *(T. montana)* has very hairy, erect seedpods. The shorter *T. rhombifolia* has pods that are bent down and often curved into the shape of a half-circle.

Golden Banner

H. WAYNE PHILLIPS

Golden Smoke

GOLDEN SMOKE
Corydalis aurea
Fumitory family (Fumariaceae)

Description: Clusters of yellow flowers lay amid lacy, fernlike leaves. The ½–¾" long, 4-petalled blossoms have 2 outer petals (the upper one is spurred) and 2 inner petals that are joined at the top. There are 2 tiny sepals, which fall off early, and 6 stamens. Smooth, 3–6" long leaves are twice pinnately divided. Narrow, slightly curved pods are ¾–1" long. This branched, 4–16" plant usually grows in low clumps.

Early spring to late summer.

Habitat/Range: Found on gravelly slopes, disturbed ground, and along streams and roads in the foothills, montane, and lower subalpine ecosystems from Alaska to New Mexico.

Comments: Also called Scrambled Eggs. This plant is related to Western Bleeding Heart *(Dicentra formosa),* Dutchman's Breeches *(D. cucullaria),* Steershead *(D. uniflora),* and Squirrel Corn *(D. canadensis).*

AVALANCHE LILY
Erythronium grandiflorum
Lily family (Liliaceae)

Description: Exquisite bright yellow blossoms with curved-back tepals dangle from slender stems. There usually are 1–5 flowers on each smooth stalk. Showy golden or red stamens protrude from the blossoms. The 2 smooth basal leaves are 4–9¾" long. The shiny green leaves are oblong and have parallel veins. The fruit is a 3-sided capsule. These showy plants often grow in groups and are 6–15" tall.

Early spring to midsummer.

Habitat/Range: Found at moist edges of snowbanks as well as in meadows, forests, and near streams in the foothills, montane, subalpine, and alpine ecosystems from Canada to Colorado.

Comments: Also called Snow Lily, Glacier Lily, Fawn Lily, Adders-Tongue, or Dogtooth Violet. Members of many different Native American nations cooked and ate the bulbs.

Avalanche Lily

Linearleaf Blazing Star

LINEARLEAF BLAZING STAR
Nuttalia speciosa
Blazing Star family (Loasaceae)

Description: Golden or lemony yellow, star-like flowers grow atop slender stems. The 1½–2" wide blossoms have 10 petals and many tall stamens. The alternate leaves bear rough, hooked hairs that stick to clothing. The simple upper leaves are very slender and toothed. The seedpods look like goblets or wide champagne flutes. The stems are branched and grow 1–2' tall.

Early to late summer.

Habitat/Range: Found in sandy fields, disturbed sites, and along roads in the foothills and montane ecosystems from Wyoming to New Mexico.

Comments: Also called Stickleaf or Yellow Evening Star, formerly *Mentzelia aurea* or *speciosa* because the flowers bloom in the evening. White Blazing Star is a common white-flowered species within this genus.

Yellow Pondlily

YELLOW PONDLILY
Nuphar lutea ssp. *polysepala*
Water Lily family (Nymphaeaceae)

Description: Waxy, cup-shaped yellow flowers are 3–5½" wide. Blossoms usually have 9 yellow sepals, which may be tinted with red, and small petals that are the same length as the many stamens. Numerous pistils share a fleshy base. Flowers are on stalks just above the water, or they float on the water's surface like the leathery leaves. The simple, entire leaves are oval, round, or heart-shaped, 4–12" long, with long underwater stalks. This perennial has a somewhat egg-shaped fruit that is 1" in diameter.

Late spring to late summer.

Habitat/Range: Found sporadically in montane and subalpine ponds, lakes, and calmer streams from Alaska to Colorado.

Comments: Also called Spatterdock or Wokas. Klamath Indians ate the roasted seeds or made bread and porridge from the ground seeds. Beavers and muskrats eat the scaly yellow roots.

COMMON EVENING PRIMROSE
Oenothera villosa
Evening Primrose family (Onagraceae)

Description: These yellow flowers bloom for one evening and then fade to orange. The 4 petals are less than 1" long and open in the late afternoon. The blossoms have 8 stamens, a 4-parted stigma, and 4 bent-back sepals. Alternate, 1–4" long leaves are hairy and usually entire. The erect, 1–3¼' stem is covered with stiff hairs.

Mid- to late summer.

Habitat/Range: Common in disturbed sites and along roads and trails in the foothills and montane ecosystems from Montana to Colorado.

Comments: Formerly known by the scientific name *O. strigosa.* Yellow Evening Primrose *(O. flava)* is a very low plant with toothed or lobed leaves.

Common Evening Primrose

Yellow Ladyslipper

YELLOW LADYSLIPPER
Cypripedium calceolus ssp. *parviflorum*
Orchid family (Orchidaceae)

Description: A single, moccasin-shaped flower dangles from an erect stem. The yellow lower petal forms a sac-shaped lip and is ¾–2" long. Reddish purple dots mark the inside of this fragrant blossom. There also are 2 twisted, reddish tan or yellowish green petals and 3 similar sepals. There usually are 3–5 alternate leaves that are 3–6" long. Sticky hairs cover the leaves. The stout, hairy stem is 8–22" tall.

Late spring to late summer.

Habitat/Range: This rare plant is found in moist aspen forests, in marshes, along streams, and bordering ponds in the foothills, montane, and subalpine ecosystems from Canada to New Mexico.

Comments: Also called Moccasin Flower and Small Lady's Slipper. Some botanists place this species in the Ladyslipper family (Cypripediaceae).

Sulphur Flower

SULPHUR FLOWER
Eriogonum umbellatum
Buckwheat family (Polygonaceae)

Description: Small bright yellow flowers are grouped in ball-like clusters. The clusters sit atop stalks that all originate from 1 point; just below this point are several leafy bracts. Each flower has 6 petal-like sepals that turn reddish brown as they age. A basal rosette contains oval or spoon-shaped leaves that are ¼–2" long with fuzzy hairs on the undersurface. The small seeds are not winged. This mat-forming perennial grows 4–12" in height.
Early to late summer.

Habitat/Range: Found in fields, forest openings, on slopes, and along roads in the foothills, montane, and subalpine ecosystems from Canada to Arizona.

Comments: The generic name *Eriogonum* means "woolly knee." This refers to the woolly stems of some species.

SAGEBRUSH BUTTERCUP
Ranunculus glaberrimus var. *ellipticus*
Buttercup family (Ranunculaceae)

Description: Typically, 5–8 shiny yellow petals surround numerous stamens. The ¾–1¼" wide blossoms have lavender-tinted sepals. Long-stemmed basal leaves are round or elliptic. The smooth, ½–2" long leaves are entire and fleshy. Some of the stem leaves have 3 lobes. This perennial grows to 2–8" in height and usually has a reclining stem.
Early spring to early summer.

Habitat/Range: Found in fields of sagebrush, on moist hillsides, and in sunny pine forests in the foothills and montane ecosystems from Canada to New Mexico.

Comments: Also called Early Buttercup or Crowfoot. *Ranunculus* means "little frog"; many of the species in this genus grow in wet areas.

Sagebrush Buttercup

SNOW BUTTERCUP
Ranunculus adoneus
Buttercup family (Ranunculaceae)

Description: From 1–3 showy yellow flowers usually appear before the leaves unfurl. The ⅜–1½" wide blossoms have shiny petals and hairy sepals. The leaves have 3 lobes, each of which is twice divided into narrow segments. The smooth stems grow 4–12" and the plants often appear in clusters.

Early to late summer.

Habitat/Range: Found circling melting snowbanks, in wet meadows, and near streams in the upper subalpine and alpine ecosystems from Wyoming to Colorado and from Idaho to Nevada.

Comments: Also called Alpine Buttercup. A similar species, Subalpine Buttercup *(R. eschscholtzii)*, has 3-lobed leaves with entire or once-divided segments.

Snow Buttercup

ROCKY MOUNTAIN NATIONAL PARK

Alpine Avens

ALPINE AVENS
Acomastylis rossii ssp. *turbinata*
Rose family (Rosaceae)

Description: The 5 bright yellow petals surround the numerous stamens of this ¾" wide flower. The 5 sepals often are purple-tinged. Fernlike, 2–6" long leaves are mainly basal. The deep green leaves are pinnately divided into 9–33 toothed leaflets. These and the 1–3 stem leaves turn red in fall. In the summer, this 3–12" plant often forms a yellow-and-green carpet on the alpine tundra.

Early to late summer.

Habitat/Range: Very common in meadows and gravelly areas of the subalpine and alpine ecosystems from Alaska to New Mexico.

Comments: Also called Ross's Avens, formerly *Geum rossii* var. *turbinatum*. The specific name honors the Arctic explorer James Ross. Cinquefoils *(Potentilla)* look similar, but their basal leaves usually have 3–13 leaflets and may be palmately compound.

Beauty Cinquefoil

BEAUTY CINQUEFOIL
Potentilla pulcherrima
Rose family (Rosaceae)

Description: These bright yellow, ½–¾" flowers sit atop branched stems. The 5 petals often are decorated with an orange spot at the base. The mainly basal leaves have long stalks. They may be palmately or pinnately compound with narrow leaflets. The 5–11 leaflets are green above and have white woolly hairs below. Slender stems are 1–2' high.

Early to late summer.

Habitat/Range: Found in meadows, open forests, on moist hillsides, or near streams in the foothills, montane, subalpine, and alpine ecosystems from Alaska to Colorado.

Comments: Also called Fivefinger, formerly *P. gracilis* or *P. filipes*. The cinquefoils may be hard to identify since they interbreed, creating hybrids with intermediate characteristics.

LEAFY CINQUEFOIL
Drymocallis fissa
Rose family (Rosaceae)

Description: The flowers are ¾–1" wide, typically yellow or occasionally creamy white, and appear in narrow clusters. The 5 petals usually are longer than the 5 sepals. The short-stalked basal leaves are pinnately compound with 9–13 broad, oval-shaped leaflets. The bottom leaflets are smallest and usually have some sticky hairs. Stem leaves are smaller. Leafy, sticky stems most often are 8–12" tall and have a reddish color.

Late spring to late summer.

Habitat/Range: Common in meadows, in open forests, on rocky hillsides, and along roads in the foothills, montane, and subalpine ecosystems from Wyoming to New Mexico.

Comments: Also called Wood Beauty, formerly *Potentilla fissa, P. glandulosa* or *P. scopulorum. Cinquefoil* is a French word meaning "5 leaves" as some species have 5 leaflets.

DENVER BOTANIC GARDENS

Leafy Cinquefoil

SHRUBBY CINQUEFOIL
Pentaphylloides floribunda
Rose family (Rosaceae)

Description: This shrub often is covered with 5-petaled yellow blossoms that have many stamens. The 1–1½" wide flowers have 5 sepals. The pinnately compound leaves usually are less than 1½" long. The 3–7 narrow, entire leaflets are covered with gray hairs on the lower surface. The bark is brownish, peeling, and lacks thorns. The bottom section of the branched stems is woody. This plant grows 4–39" tall.

Early summer to early fall.

Habitat/Range: Found in moist meadows, open woods, and on hillsides in the foothills, montane, subalpine, and alpine ecosystems from Alaska to New Mexico.

Comments: Also called Yellow Rose, formerly *Potentilla fruticosa.* The generic name *Pentaphylloides* means "5 leaves" as there usually are 5 leaflets. Varieties of this shrub often are used in yards and gardens.

LORAINE YEATTS

Shrubby Cinquefoil

Bracted Lousewort

BRACTED LOUSEWORT
Pedicularis bracteosa ssp. *paysoniana*
Snapdragon family (Scrophulariaceae)

Description: Yellowish flowers 1" long are arranged in a dense cluster with leafy green bracts. The blossoms are 2-lipped with the top lip arched and the bottom lip 3-lobed. Most of the stalked leaves grow from the hairy stem. The 2–6" long leaves are pinnately divided into toothed, fernlike leaflets. This perennial has several unbranched stems that grow 1–3' tall.
Early to late summer.

Habitat/Range: Found in forests, shady meadows, and on rocky hillsides in the montane and subalpine ecosystems from Montana to Colorado.

Comments: Also called Wood Betony, Towering Lousewort, or Fernleaf Lousewort. Giant Lousewort *(P. procera)* has longer leaves and flowers with reddish purple streaks. The yellow- or reddish-flowered Canada Lousewort *(P. canadensis)* has simple leaves that are not deeply lobed.

NORTHERN PAINTBRUSH
Castilleja sulphurea
Snapdragon family (Scrophulariaceae)

Description: Sticky hairs adorn the clusters of yellow or whitish sepals and bracts that hide inconspicuous flowers. The 1" long blossoms have an upper yellow petal; the lower petal looks like a green bump. The leaves are 1–3" long, usually smooth and entire, lance-shaped, and have 3–5 main veins. The stems often are branched once and grow in clumps. The plants are 12–20" tall, but sometimes shorter.
Late spring to late summer.

Habitat/Range: Common in moist aspen forests, in shady meadows, and near streams in the foothills, montane, and subalpine ecosystems from Canada to New Mexico.

Comments: Also called Yellow Paintbrush, formerly *C. septentrionalis.* The similar Western Yellow Paintbrush *(C. occidentalis)* has a shorter, unbranched stem. The yellow-flowered Alpine Paintbrush *(C. puberula)* is covered with woolly hairs.

ROCKY MOUNTAIN NATIONAL PARK

Northern Paintbrush

WESTERN YELLOW PAINTBRUSH
Castilleja occidentalis
Snapdragon family (Scrophulariaceae)

Description: Greenish flowers are tucked among showier, hairy bracts that are greenish yellow. The bracts are entire or may have shallow lobes. The leaves usually are entire, 1-2" long, and lance-shaped. Several unbranched stems often grow together in a clump. Grows 2-10" tall.

Midsummer.

Haibtat/Range: Common in meadows in the subalpine and alpine ecosystems from Colorado to New Mexico.

Comments: This species is shorter than the yellow-flowered Northern Paintbrush *(C. sulphurea).* The flowers of Alpine Paintbrush *(C. puberula)* have a longer lower tip and the leaves are narrower.

Western Yellow Paintbrush

GLOSSARY

Alternate – placed singly along a stem or axis, one after another, usually each successive item on a different side from the previous; often used in reference to the arrangement of leaves on a stem (see **Opposite**) (see illustration p. 16).

Angular – having angles or sharp corners; generally used in reference to stems, as contrasted with round stems.

Annual – a plant completing its life cycle, from seed germination to production of new seeds, within a year and then dying.

Awn – a slender, stiff bristle or fiber attached at its base to another part, such as a leaf tip.

Axil – the site where a leaf joins the stem.

Basal – at the base or bottom of; generally used in reference to leaves.

Biennial – a plant that completes its life cycle in two years; normally not producing flowers during the first year.

Boreal – northern.

Bract – a reduced or modified leaf, often associated with flowers.

Bractlet – a small bract.

Bristle – a stiff hair, usually erect or curving away from its attachment point.

Bulb – an underground plant part derived from a short, usually rounded shoot that is covered with scales or leaves.

Calyx – the outer set of flower parts, composed of the sepals, which may be separate or joined together; usually green.

Capsule – a dry fruit that releases seeds through splits or holes.

Circumboreal – found around the world at high latitudes or elevations.

Circumpolar – found around the world in alpine or polar regions.

Clasping – surrounding or partially wrapping around a stem or branch.

Cluster – any grouping or close arrangement of individual flowers that is not dense and continuous.

Compound Leaf – a leaf that is divided into two or more leaflets, each of which may look like a complete leaf but which lacks buds; may have leaflets arranged along an axis, like the rays of a feather, or radiating from a common point, like the fingers on a hand (see illustration p. 16).

Conifer – a cone-bearing tree or shrub, usually evergreen.

Corm – an enlarged base or stem resembling a bulb.

Corolla – the set of flower parts interior to the calyx and surrounding the stamens, composed of the petals which may be free or united; often brightly colored.

Disk Flower – a small, tubular flower in the central portion of the flower head of many plants in the Aster family (Asteraceae) (see illustration p. 20).

Disturbed – referring to habitats that have been impacted by actions or processes associated with European settlement such as ditching, grading, or long intervals of high-intensity grazing.

Draw – a small, elongated depression with

gentle side slopes in an upland landscape; resembles a miniature valley or ravine.

Ecosystem – a recognizable community of plants and animals affected by environmental factors such as elevation, wind, temperature, precipitation, sunlight, soil type, and direction of slope.

Entire – a leaf edge that is smooth, without teeth or notches.

Erect – upright, standing vertically, or directly perpendicular from a surface.

Escape – referring to plants that have been cultivated in an area and spread from there into the wild.

Family – a group of plants having biologically similar features such as flower anatomy, fruit type, etc.

Fellfield – a tundra area comprised greatly of broken rock, possibly interspersed with accumulations of soils and plant life.

Fen – a specialized wetland permanently supplied with mineralized groundwater.

Flower Head – as used in this guide, a dense and continuous group of flowers without obvious branches or space between them; used especially in reference to the Aster family (Asteraceae).

Generic Name – the first portion of a scientific name, identifying a particular species; for instance in Colorado Columbine, *Aquilegia coerula*, the generic name is *Aquilegia* (see **Specific Name**).

Genus – a group of closely related species such as the genus *Viola*, encompassing the violets.

Gland – a bump, projection, or round protuberance, usually colored differently than the object on which it occurs; often sticky or producing sticky or oily secretions.

Herbaceous – fleshy-stemmed; not woody.

Hood – a curving or folded, petal-like structure interior to the petals and exterior to the stamens in certain flowers, including in milkweeds. Since most milkweeds have bent-back petals, the hoods typically are the most prominent feature of the flowers.

Hooded – arching over and partially concealing or shielding.

Horn – a small, round, or flattened projection from the hoods of milkweed flowers.

Host – as used here, a plant from which a parasitic plant derives nourishment.

Infusion – a tealike beverage made by steeping plant parts (usually leaves) in hot water.

Keel – a pair of united petals present in pea and other flowers.

Lance-shaped – shaped like the head of a lance or spear.

Leaflet – a distinct, leaflike segment of a compound leaf.

Ligule – a protruding, often scalelike structure at the base of the leaf blade in many grasses and some sedges.

Lobe – a segment of an incompletely divided plant part, typically rounded; often used in reference to leaves.

Margin – the edge of a leaf or petal.

Mat – densely interwoven or tangled, low plant growth.

Mesic – referring to a habitat that is well-drained, but generally moist throughout most of the growing season.

Opposite – paired directly across from one another along a stem or axis (see **Alternate**) (see illustration p. 16).

Ovary – the portion of the flower where the seeds develop, usually a swollen area below the style (if present) and stigma.

Ovate – egg-shaped.

Palmate – spreading like the fingers of a hand (see illustration p. 16).

Parallel – side by side, approximately the same distance apart, for the entire length; often used in reference to veins or edges of leaves.

Perennial – a plant that normally lives for three or more years.

Petal – the component parts of the corolla, often the most brightly colored and visible parts of the flower.

Pinnate – divided or lobed along each side of a leaf stalk, resembling a feather (see illustration p. 16).

Pistil – the seed-producing, or female, unit of a flower; consists of the ovary, style (if present), and stigma; a flower may have one to several separate pistils.

Pod – a dry fruit that splits open along the edges.

Pollen – tiny, often powdery, male reproductive cells formed in the stamens; typically necessary for seed production.

Prickle – a small, sharp, spinelike outgrowth from the outer surface.

Raceme – an unbranched stem with stalked flowers, the newest flowers forming at the top.

Ray Flower – a flower in the Aster family (Asteraceae) with a single, strap-shaped corolla resembling one flower petal; ray flowers may surround the disk flowers in a flower head, or in some species such as dandelions, the flower heads may be composed entirely of ray flowers (see illustration p. 20).

Resinous – containing or covered with sticky to semisolid, clearish sap or gum.

Rhizome – an underground stem producing roots and shoots at the nodes.

Runner – a long, trailing stem.

Sap – the juice within a plant.

Sedge – a large group of grasslike plants, many of which grow in wetlands.

Seepage – referring to an area with small volumes of subsurface water supply.

Sepal – a component part of the calyx; typically green but sometimes enlarged and brightly colored.

Serrate – possessing sharp, forward-pointing teeth.

Shrub – a small, multistemmed, woody plant.

Simple Leaf – a leaf that has a single leaflike blade, although this may be lobed or divided (see illustration p. 16).

Specific Epithet – see **Specific Name.**

Specific Name – the second portion of a scientific name, identifying a particular species; for instance in Colorado Columbine, *Aquilegia coerula*, the specific name is *coerula*.

Spike – an elongated, unbranched cluster of stalkless or nearly stalkless flowers.

Spine – a thin, stiff, sharply pointed projection.

Spreading – extending outward from; at right angles to; widely radiating.

Spur – a hollow, tubular projection from the base of a petal or sepal; often produces nectar.

Stalk – as used here, the stem supporting the leaf, flower, or flower cluster.

Stalkless – lacking a stalk. A stalkless leaf is attached directly to the stem at the leaf base.

Stamen – the male unit of a flower which produces the pollen; typically consisting of a long filament with a pollen-producing tip.

Standard – the usually erect, spreading upper petal in many flowers of the Bean family (Fabaceae).

Sterile – in flowers, referring to an inability to produce seeds; in habitats, referring to poor nutrient and mineral availability in the soil.

Stigma – the portion of the pistil receptive to pollination; usually at the top of the style, and often appearing fuzzy or sticky.

Stipule – a bract or leafy structure occurring in pairs at the base of the leaf stalk.

Style – the portion of the pistil between the ovary and the stigma; typically a slender stalk.

Subspecies – a group of plants within a species that has consistent, repeating, genetic, and structural distinctions.

Succulent – thickened and fleshy or juicy.

Swale – a depression or shallow hollow in the

land, typically moist.

Taproot – a stout, main root extending downward.

Tepals – petals and sepals that cannot be distinguished from each other.

Toothed – bearing teeth or sharply angled projections along the edge.

Tuber – a thick, creeping underground stem; sometimes also used to describe thickened portions of roots.

Tubercle – a small, rounded projection, as occurs on a cactus or a plant root.

Tubular – narrow, cylindrical, and tubelike.

Variety – a group of plants within a species that has a distinct range, habitat, or structure.

Veins – bundles of small tubes that carry water, minerals, and nutrients.

Whorl – three or more parts attached at the same point along a stem or axis and often surrounding the stem.

Winged – having thin bands of leaflike tissue attached edgewise along the length.

Wings – the two side petals flanking the keel in many flowers of the Bean family (Fabaceae).

Woody – firm-stemmed or branched.

SELECTED REFERENCES

Anderson, Berta. 1976. *Wildflower Name Tales*. Colorado Springs, Colo.: Century One Press.

Carter, Jack L. 1988. *Trees and Shrubs of Colorado*. Boulder, Colo.: Johnson Books.

Coffey, Timothy. 1994. *The History and Folklore of North American Wildflowers*. Boston, Mass.: Houghton Mifflin.

Colorado Native Plant Society. 1997. *Rare Plants of Colorado*. Revised edition. Estes Park, Colo.: Rocky Mountain Nature Association; Helena, Mont.: Falcon.

Craighead, John J., Frank C. Craighead, and Ray J. Davis, 1963. *A Field Guide to Rocky Mountain Wildflowers*. Boston, Mass: Houghton Mifflin.

Duft, Joseph F. and Robert K. Mosely. 1989. *Alpine Wildflowers of the Rocky Mountains*. Missoula, Mont.: Mountain Press.

Guennel, C.K. 1995. *Guide to Colorado Wildflowers: Mountains*. Englewood, Colo.: Westcliffe Publishers.

Harrington, Harold D. 1954. *Manual of the Plants of Colorado*. Denver, Colo.: Sage Books.

Kruger, Frances Alley and Carron A. Meaney. 1995. *Explore Colorado*. Denver, Colo.: Denver Museum of Natural History; Englewood, Colo.: Westcliffe Publishers.

Mutel, Cornelia F. and John C. Emerick. 1984. *From Grassland to Glacier*. Boulder, Colo.: Johnson Books.

Nelson, Ruth Ashton. 1992. *Handbook of Rocky Mountain Plants*. Revised by Roger L. Williams. Denver, Colo.: Denver Museum of Natural History; Niwot, Colo.: Roberts Rinehart Publishers.

Pesman, M. Walter. 1992. *Meet the Natives*. Revised edition. Denver, Colo.: Denver Botanic Gardens.

Spellenberg, Richard. 1995. *National Audubon Society Field Guide to North American Wildflowers*. Revised edition. New York: Alfred A. Knopf.

Weber, W.A. and R.C. Wittmann. 1996. *Colorado Flora: Eastern Slope*. Revised edition. Niwot, Colo.: University Press of Colorado.

Weber, W.A. and R.C. Wittmann. 1996. *Colorado Flora: Western Slope*. Revised edition. Niwot, Colo.: University Press of Colorado.

Willard, Beatrice E. and M.T. Smithson. 1988. *Alpine Wildflowers of the Rocky Mountains*. Estes Park, Colo.: Rocky Mountain Nature Association.

Zwinger, Ann H. and Beatrice E. Willard. 1989. *Land Above the Trees*. Tucson, Ariz.: University of Arizona.

INDEX

About the Author

Writer/interpreter Leigh Robertson gained her extensive knowledge of Rocky Mountain wildflowers while working for the USDA Forest Service, The Nature Conservancy, Flathead Lake Biological Station, and various city, county, and state parks. She recently served as interpretive program supervisor for the City of Colorado Springs, Colorado, at Garden of the Gods Park and Pikes Peak. Robertson lives in Woodland Park, Colorado.

Rocky Mountain Nature Association

Founded in 1931, the nonprofit Rocky Mountain Nature Association (RMNA) assists Rocky Mountain National Park, Florissant National Monument, USDA Forest Service, the Bureau of Land Management, Colorado state parks, and the City of Colorado Springs by providing interpretive materials for visitors. RMNA is a major contributor to improvement projects, educational programs, research efforts, and critical land acquisitions.

For the latest RMNA mail order catalog, call 800-816-7662.

FALCON GUIDES ® Leading the Way

FIELD GUIDES

Bitterroot: Montana State Flower
Canyon Country Wildflowers
Central Rocky Mountains
    Wildflowers
Great Lakes Berry Book
New England Berry Book
Ozark Wildflowers
Pacific Northwest Berry Book
Plants of Arizona
Rare Plants of Colorado
Rocky Mountain Berry Book
Scats & Tracks of the Pacific
    Coast States
Scats & Tracks of the
    Rocky Mountains
Southern Rocky Mountain
    Wildflowers
Tallgrass Prairie Wildflowers
Western Trees
Wildflowers of Southwestern
    Utah
Willow Bark and Rosehips

FISHING GUIDES

Fishing Alaska
Fishing the Beartooths
Fishing Florida
Fishing Glacier National Park
Fishing Maine
Fishing Montana
Fishing Wyoming
Fishing Yellowstone
    National Park

ROCKHOUNDING GUIDES

Rockhounding Arizona
Rockhounding California
Rockhounding Colorado
Rockhounding Montana
Rockhounding Nevada
Rockhound's Guide to New
    Mexico
Rockhounding Texas
Rockhounding Utah
Rockhounding Wyoming

MORE GUIDEBOOKS

Backcountry Horseman's
    Guide to Washington
Camping California's
    National Forests
Exploring Canyonlands &
    Arches National Parks
Exploring Hawaii's Parklands
Exploring Mount Helena
Exploring Southern California
    Beaches
Recreation Guide to WA
    National Forests
Touring California & Nevada
    Hot Springs
Touring Colorado Hot Springs
Touring Montana & Wyoming
    Hot Springs
Trail Riding Western
    Montana
Wild Country Companion
Wilderness Directory
Wild Montana
Wild Utah

BIRDING GUIDES

Birding Minnesota
Birding Montana
Birding Northern California
Birding Texas
Birding Utah

PADDLING GUIDES

Floater's Guide to Colorado
Paddling Minnesota
Paddling Montana
Paddling Okefenokee
Paddling Oregon
Paddling Yellowstone & Grand
    Teton National Parks

HOW-TO GUIDES

Avalanche Aware
Backpacking Tips
Bear Aware
Desert Hiking Tips
Hiking with Dogs
Leave No Trace
Mountain Lion Alert
Reading Weather
Route Finding
Using GPS
Wilderness First Aid
Wilderness Survival

WALKING

Walking Colorado Springs
Walking Denver
Walking Portland
Walking St. Louis
Walking Virginia Beach

■ *To order any of these books, check with your local bookseller
or call FALCON ® at **1-800-582-2665.**
Visit us on the world wide web at:*
www.FalconOutdoors.com

Leading the Way

Come to America's wilderness areas and enjoy some of the most pristine hiking conditions you'll ever experience. With FalconGuides® you'll be able to plan your trip, including learning how to get there, getting a permit, if necessary, and picking your campsites. Types of trails, difficulty ratings, distances, maps, elevation charts, and backcountry regulations are covered in detail. You'll also learn "leave no trace" principles, safety tips, and other essential information specific to the wilderness area you visit. The following titles are currently available, and this list grows every year. For a free catalog with a complete list of titles, call FALCON toll-free at 800-582-2665.

Hiking the Beartooths
Hiking the Bob Marshall Country
Hiking Colorado's Weminuche Wilderness
Hiking Oregon's Central Cascades
Hiking Oregon's Eagle Cap Wilderness
Hiking Oregon's Mount Hood & Badger Creek Wilderness
Hiking Wyoming's Cloud Peak Wilderness
Hiking Wyoming's Wind River Range
Wild Montana
Wild Utah

Wilderness area FalconGuides® are
published in cooperation with
The Wilderness Society

To order any of these books, check with your local bookseller,
Or call FALCON at 1-800-582-2665.
Visit us on the world wide web at:
www.FalconOutdoors.com

Going Somewhere?

Insiders' Guides offer 60 current and upcoming titles to some of the country's most popular vacation destinations (including the ones listed below), and we're adding many more. Written by local authors and averaging 400 pages, our guides provide the information you need quickly and easily—whether searching for savory local cuisine, unique regional wares, amusements for the kids, a picturesque hiking spot, off-the-beaten-track attractions, new environs or a room with a view.

Explore America and experience the joy of travel with the Insiders' Guide® books.

Adirondacks
Atlanta, GA
Austin, TX
Baltimore
Bend & Central Oregon
Bermuda
Boca Raton & the Palm Beaches
Boise & Sun Valley
Boulder & the Rocky Mountain National Park
Branson & the Ozark Mountains
California's Wine Country
Cape Cod, Nantucket and Martha's Vineyard
Charleston, SC
Cincinnati
Civil War Sites in the Eastern Theater
Colorado's Mountains
Denver
The Florida Keys & Key West
Florida's Great Northwest
Golf in the Carolinas
Indianapolis
The Lake Superior Region
Las Vegas
Lexington, KY
Louisville, KY
Madison, WI
Maine's Mid-Coast
Maine's Southern Coast
Michigan's Traverse Bay Region
Mississippi

Montana's Glacier Country
Monterey Peninsula
Myrtle Beach
Nashville
New Hampshire
North Carolina's Central Coast & New Bern
North Carolina's Southern Coast & Wilmington
North Carolina's Mountains
North Carolina's Outer Banks
Phoenix
The Pocono Mountains
Portland
Relocation
Richmond
Salt Lake City
San Diego
Santa Barbara
Santa Fe
Sarasota & Bradenton
Savannah
Southwestern Utah
Tampa & St. Petersburg
Texas Coastal Bend
Tucson
Twin Cities
Virginia's Blue Ridge
Virginia's Chesapeake Bay
Washington, D.C.
Williamsburg
Yellowstone

FALCONGUIDES® Leading the Way

WILDLIFE VIEWING GUIDES

Alaska Wildlife Viewing Guide
Arizona Wildlife Viewing Guide
California Wildlife Viewing Guide
Colorado Wildlife Viewing Guide
Florida Wildlife Viewing Guide
Indiana Wildlife Vewing Guide
Iowa Wildlife Viewing Guide
Kentucky Wildlife Viewing Guide
Massachusetts Wildlife Viewing Guide
Montana Wildlife Viewing Guide
Nebraska Wildlife Viewing Guide
Nevada Wildlife Viewing Guide
New Hampshire Wildlife Viewing Guide
New Jersey Wildlife Viewing Guide
New Mexico Wildlife Viewing Guide
New York Wildlife Viewing Guide
North Carolina Wildlife Viewing Guide
North Dakota Wildlife Viewing Guide
Ohio Wildlife Viewing Guide
Oregon Wildlife Viewing Guide
Puerto Rico and the Virgin Islands WVG
Tennessee Wildlife Viewing Guide
Texas Wildlife Viewing Guide
Utah Wildlife Viewing Guide
Vermont Wildlife Viewing Guide
Virginia Wildlife Viewing Guide
Washington Wildlife Viewing Guide
West Virginia Wildlife Viewing Guide
Wisconsin Wildlife Viewing Guide

HISTORIC TRAIL GUIDES

Traveling California's Gold Rush Country
Traveling the Lewis & Clark Trail
Traveling the Oregon Trail
Traveler's Guide to the Pony Express Trail

SCENIC DRIVING GUIDES

Scenic Driving Alaska and the Yukon
Scenic Driving Arizona
Scenic Driving the Beartooth Highway
Scenic Driving California
Scenic Driving Colorado
Scenic Driving Florida
Scenic Driving Georgia
Scenic Driving Hawaii
Scenic Driving Idaho
Scenic Driving Michigan
Scenic Driving Minnesota
Scenic Driving Montana
Scenic Driving New England
Scenic Driving New Mexico
Scenic Driving North Carolina
Scenic Driving Oregon
Scenic Driving the Ozarks including the
   Ouchita Mountains
Scenic Driving Pennsylvania
Scenic Driving Texas
Scenic Driving Utah
Scenic Driving Washington
Scenic Driving Wisconsin
Scenic Driving Wyoming
Scenic Driving Yellowstone & Grand Teton
   National Parks
Back Country Byways
Scenic Byways East
Scenic Byways Farwest
Scenic Byways Rocky Mountains

■ *To order any of these books, check with your local bookseller*
or call FALCON ® at 1-800-582-2665.
Visit us on the world wide web at:
www.FalconOutdoors.com